AIR

BRUSH

ART

THE MURAL IN AIR-BRUSH. Air-brush painting lends itself toward the modern abstraction and stylized form of composition so popular in the modern mural, as well as for the mural in the more conventional style. This is a portion of an air-brushed mural representative of progress in business and industry. The creating of air-brushed murals is described in Part 9, beginning on page 173.

AIR
BRUSH
ART

BY

GEORGE W. KADEL

THE SIGNS OF THE TIMES PUBLISHING COMPANY
CINCINNATI, OHIO

OTHER SIGNS OF THE TIMES BOOKS:

LETTERING FOR COMMERCIAL PURPOSES, BY WILLIAM HUGH GORDON

LUMINOUS ADVERTISING SKETCHES, BY PHILIP Di LEMME

MODERN BRUSH LETTERING, BY HAROLD HOLLAND DAY

SCREEN PROCESS PRICE LISTS, BY HARRY L. HIETT

MODERN ORNAMENT AND DESIGN, BY J. N. HALSTED

SCREEN PROCESS PRODUCTION, BY HARRY L. HIETT

SIMPLIFIED SHOW CARD WRITING, BY TOM KELLEY

ALPHABETS AND LAYOUTS, BY AL. IMELLI

SHOW CARD LAYOUTS, BY H. C. MARTIN

POSTER ART, BY DUKE WELLINGTON

STANDARD PRICE GUIDE

CONTENTS

PART IV—PORTRAITS

PART V—FASHION ART

PART VI—ILLUSTRATIONS

PART VII—ARCHITECTURAL DRAWINGS

PART VIII—PHOTOGRAPH RETOUCHING

PART IX—THE MURAL

PART X—FLOCKING WITH THE AIR BRUSH

CONCLUSION

PART I

THE ARTIST AND THE AIR BRUSH

CHAPTER I

AIR BRUSH ART

WEBSTER states that an air brush is "a kind of atomizer for applying liquid coloring matter in a spray by compressed air." This concise definition is far from conveying to the layman and even to the average artist the innumerable possibilities that the air brush possesses in the realm of art, from the embellishing of furniture to the rendering of paintings in the fine arts.

THE AIR BRUSH IN MODERN USAGE. One reason for this lack of understanding of the full scope of service that is possible with the air brush seems to have been the absence of adequate instructions and informative suggestions presented in book form. Within recent years, since many new uses for the air brush in art have been put into practice and since numerous advancements have been made in the manufacture of air-brush equipment, there has been no extensive literature, save in periodicals, on the adaptability of the air brush to modern usage.

PRACTICAL INSTRUCTION NEEDED. My work of instructing artists and art students in this modern usage of the air brush has convinced me more than anything else could of the urgent need for such a book by artists, schools, colleges, display men, and others interested in learning or teaching air-brush art, particularly in practical application to commercial art, fashion art, retouching, and advertising display. I have therefore prepared this book, which I feel, from my own experiences, should serve as a course in practical air-brush art instruction, such as I have used in my own classes.

THE MODERN AIR BRUSH. The modern air brushes are naturally far more perfect instruments of art than were the first air brushes, which were made in the early part of the 1890s. Then the air brush was a mechanical tool more than an instrument of art. Its chief use

9

then was to produce novel sprayed effects that today would seem indeed to be crude forerunners of the beautiful, exact, and delicate renderings that are possible with the modern air brush in the hands of a practiced artist.

ITS POSSIBILITIES. The air brush, used in the many fields of creative art, makes possible the achievement of artistic effects that are attainable in no other way, from the most delicate traceries to the solid wash. For painting, coloring, drawing, retouching, and decorating, the air brush is being used more and more to achieve an individualized treatment in the many forms of art. Remarkable as the statement seems, it is no exaggeration to say that the air brush can be employed to advantage in every form of art that is in use today.

The speed with which the accomplished air-brush artist can work is one of the chief advantages in using the air brush at a time when rapid execution of art creations is more and more in demand. Air-brushed art is the answer in this day of speed, when in some branches of commercial art the production of art work must be completed on extremely short notice.

ITS APPLICATIONS. It is well to view at the outset some of the many kinds of art work to which the air brush can be applied. The following list is by no means a complete one, but it serves to convey an idea of the extensiveness of air-brush work in present-day applications. It also serves as an index of the kinds of air-brush work you can do if you follow with diligence and perseverence the instructions given in this book. The art applications include the making, embellishing, or treating of (as the case may be) the following:

Advertising Displays	Advertisement Illustrations
Architectural Drawing	Calendars
Candles	Candlesticks
Car Cards	Catalog Illustrating
Clothing Drawings	Covers for Books
Decalcomanias	Decorations
Display Backgrounds	Dioramas
Enlargements	Exhibits
Fashion Illustrating	Fine Art
Fixtures for Displays	Fresco Work
Furniture	Games

Greeting Cards	Jackets for Books
Jewelry Drawings	Label Designs
Lamps	Leather Novelties
Letterheads	Lettering
Lithography	Machinery Drawings
Magazine Illustrating	Mannikins
Moving-Picture Film	Monument Drawings
Negative Retouching	Newspaper Illustrating
Package Designing	Paintings
Photo Retouching	Portraits
Posters	Scenery
Screen Process Work	Shoe Drawings
Shoe Decorations	Signs
Sign Sketches	Statuary
Tapestries	Textiles
Titles for Motion Pictures	Toys
Wall Hangings	Wall Paper Designing

STUDY AND PRACTICE. The degree of your proficiency in using the air brush is commensurate first with your knowledge of the various air-brushed treatments based on the fundamentals of form representation and shading, and second with your ability to apply that knowledge in your work as the occasion demands.

The attaining of a high degree of proficiency therefore requires thorough study and correct practice.

MASTER FUNDAMENTALS FIRST. The mere reading of this text will not make the reader a professional air-brush artist; it must be studied, and the study must be accompanied by the actual handling of the air brush, as prescribed, for example, in the chapters on air-brush drills and form representation. Eagerness to proceed with the making of actual air-brushed renderings must not be permitted to cause the fundamentals to be hastily and inadequately learned. Have a firm foundation for your structure of knowledge and you will be enabled to scale its heights with your later acquired ability.

CHAPTER II

USING THE AIR BRUSH

THE AIR-BRUSH USER should bear in mind the functions of the air brush according to which all air-brush work can be classified. These functions are the producing of outlining and shading, special textures, novel designs and effects, and careful representations of reflected light and color on the various forms and shapes reproduced in illustrative work, decorative work, and modern advertising display, all of which the practiced air-brush artist should be able to accomplish with reasonable speed and ease.

SELECTING THE AIR BRUSH. The fineness of line desired and the size of the work to be air-brushed are the governing factors in the selecting of the type of air brush most suitable for the performing of the particular functions required of it. Renderings that require delicate outlining and extremely subtle shadings necessitate the use of a delicately adjusted and sensitive air brush. Extremely delicate illustrating and photograph retouching require an air brush capable of producing hair-line detail and of atomizing fairly heavy solutions of retouching color.

If the work to be air-painted is bold and large, an air brush is needed that produces a large spray pattern and that is equipped with a color container of sufficient size to make frequent refillings unnecessary. An air brush suitable for working on a small scale is inadequate for large display work. The use of heavy color mixtures, such as show-card colors and oil colors, calls for a heavy and sturdy type of air brush that is capable of satisfactorily atomizing those mixtures.

The manufacturers of air brushes offer types of instruments to meet the various requirements, each type being best adapted to a certain range of work according to kind and size. Studying the catalogs and informative literature issued by these manufacturers is the best way for the user of the air brush to become familiar with the most recent models of air brushes that are available, as well as with the accessories and auxiliary equipment.

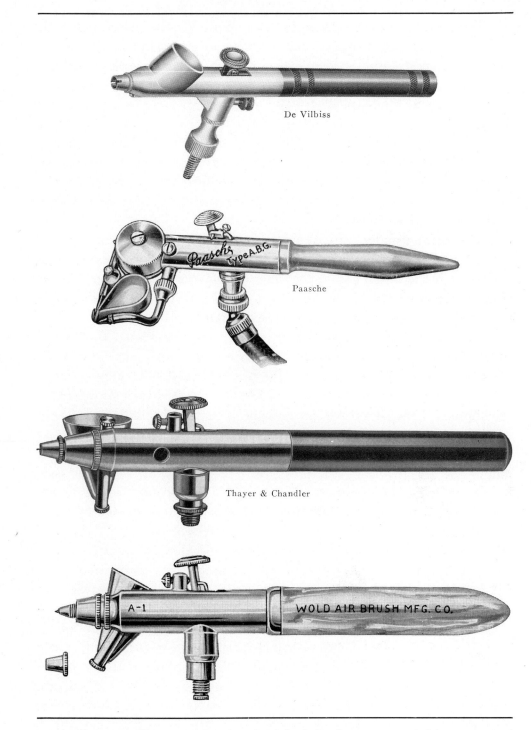

De Vilbiss

Paasche

Thayer & Chandler

AIR BRUSHES. These popular styles of artist's air brushes are some of the many types of instruments available.

THE AIR SUPPLY. Next in importance to the selection of the proper kind of air brush is the selection of the kind of air supply source that best suits the requirements of the artist's work. Carbonic gas outfits, the manually operated pump-and-tank outfit, or one of the many sizes and kinds of electrically operated air-compressor units can be used.

CARBONIC GAS OUTFITS. The carbonic gas outfit provides an inexpensive and convenient source of air that is used where electric power is not available or when an automatic compressor is not desired or required. It supplies clean air at low cost from drums rented from distributors of carbonic gas.

The outfit usually consists of an air gauge, an air regulator, wall clamp, wrench, couplings, and air hose. The regulator reduces the high pressure of the liquid gas in the drum to the working pressure desired for operation of the air brush. It is usually so arranged that a turn of a valve increases or decreases the pressure.

MANUALLY OPERATED AIR PUMPS. As the name implies, the manually operated air pumps are operated by hand or by foot as the case may be. This means that the air is forced by pumping into a reserve tank which in turn is attached to the air brush by means of air hose. This source of air supply is naturally limited to lower pressures.

AIR COMPRESSORS. Automatic electric air compressors give a sure supply of air at a constant pressure. They vary in sizes and styles to accommodate one or more air brushes. They range in size from a small, compact, portable unit that delivers twenty-five pounds of air and is operated by a one-quarter horse-power motor to a large unit that develops 150 pounds of air and is operated by a three-quarter horse-power motor. A reducer attachment supplies a continuous flow of air at a pre-determined pressure. Air storage tanks on the units supply the air in a steady flow. They also hold sufficient air in reserve so that the compressors do not have to be constantly in operation.

The smallest electrically operated compressor units are built on the old principle of the diaphragm pump. The diaphragm is constructed of composition rubber and is actuated by a piston-like rod operated from an eccentric on the motor shaft. Diaphragms will give several months of steady service, and when they are worn out, they can be easily, quickly, and inexpensively replaced. Some of these units have

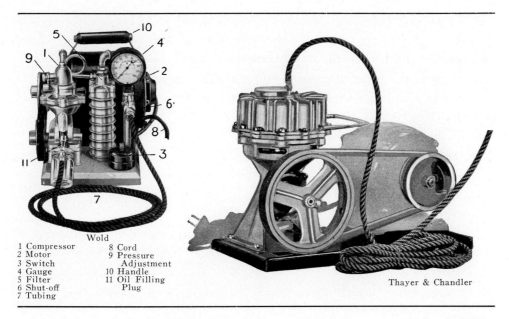

Wold

1 Compressor	8 Cord
2 Motor	9 Pressure
3 Switch	Adjustment
4 Gauge	10 Handle
5 Filter	11 Oil Filling
6 Shut-off	Plug
7 Tubing	

Thayer & Chandler

AIR COMPRESSORS. Electrically operated air compressors give a sure supply of air at a constant pressure. They vary in sizes and styles to accommodate one or more air brushes.

one diaphragm and some have two. The life of the average diaphragm rubber is usually one year.

CARE OF THE COMPRESSOR. Electrically operated compressor units are easy to install merely by attaching to an electric current outlet. They are usually of sturdy and trouble-free construction, and some models require a minimum of attention of the operator; they start and stop automatically and they are easy to regulate. All require oiling, of course, and the units must be drained regularly to remove water.

The water in the tank type of compressor should be drained from the tank each morning by opening the drain cock on the lower end of the air storage tank. The water is drained from the diaphragm type of compressor by holding the air brush open with the color cup removed.

HOLDING THE AIR BRUSH. Many students and artists who use the air brush do not hold the instrument properly to achieve the particular effects they desire. Air-brushing of extremely fine detail, such as that required in small-scale illustrating and photograph retouching, demands a sensitive control on the air-brush trigger or button.

In holding the air brush, learn to place the fingers over the instrument so that the second joint of the first finger—not the first joint—

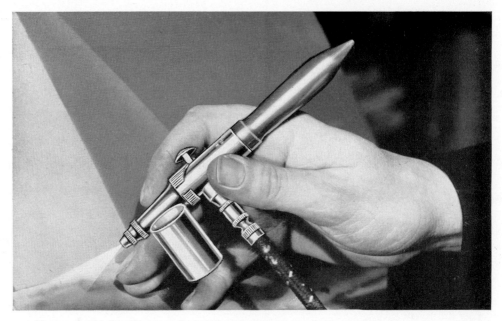

HOLDING THE AIR BRUSH. In holding the air brush, learn to place the fingers over the instrument so that the second joint of the first finger—not the first joint—operates and controls the air and color flow. Do not use the end of the finger.

operates and controls the air and color flow. Do not use the end of the finger.

Hold the air brush lightly in the hand; do not clutch it. The first thing to learn is to develop a light touch on the trigger. This alone makes possible the producing of the finest lines that can be air-brushed.

The air brush should be held at a right angle to the surface of the drawing or illustration to be painted. The tip of the air brush should be from 1/16 inch to 1½ inches away from the surface for the air-brushing of small areas and detailed designs.

SCALE OF WORKING DISTANCES. Once you have mastered a light touch on the air-brush control, the next step is to make a scale of working distances. This scale will serve as a valuable chart that will be of future assistance in determining with comparative ease the distance the air brush should be held from the work to obtain a given color value.

MAKING THE SCALE. To make the scale of working distances as accurate as possible, use a ruler to make measurements of the distances. You then will have an exact record of the tones of gray you can produce at the various distances.

Hold the ruler at a right angle to the surface on which you are to make the scale. This is the same angle at which the air brush is usually held. Set the air brush at the finest adjustment possible, hold the tip of the air brush beside the ¼ inch mark on the ruler, and apply a dot and a short line to the drawing surface.

Continue to hold the ruler in the right-angle position and lower it to a new position. This time hold the tip of the air brush beside the ½ inch mark, and again apply the dot and short line to the working surface. Repeat this same procedure at new positions with the tip of the air brush ¾ inch, 1 inch, and 1½ inches from the working surface.

WORKING DISTANCES FOR LARGE AREAS. Air-brushing of large areas requires that the working distances be greater than those considered in the preceding paragraphs. Eight to 10 inches is an ideal working distance for air-brushing a wash in a square 5 by 5 inches in size.

The air brush should be held farther from the surface of the drawing when heavy color mixtures are used than when thin mixtures are air-brushed. The color consistency must be taken into consideration, since the air brush, when held at a greater distance from the working surface, will produce a lighter tone.

CONTROLLING COLOR FLOW. It is sometimes best to use the mechanical adjustment for fixing the position of the trigger or control button on the air brush. All standard makes of air brushes are equipped with this adjustment. One make of air brush has a shoulder on the barrel, and when this shoulder is turned the position of the trigger is changed to determine the color flow. An adjustment screw on another make changes the setting of the trigger to produce a fixed and constant color flow.

SPRAY PATTERNS. The producing of spray patterns is a means of determining the consistency of the color mixture and the mechanical condition of the air brush. To make a spray pattern, hold the air brush on its side with the tip laid flat against the surface to receive the pattern. The forward part of the pattern formed when you apply the color is a parabolic curve. The rest of the pattern assumes a tear-drop shape from the tail of which springs a group of lines.

If the lines in this group are sharp and wide, the color mixture being used is too thin. If the lines are long and slender, the color mixture is of the right consistency. If the upper or lower portion of the forward curve of the pattern is flattened, the cone or the needle point on the air brush is bent and needs to be replaced in order to make possible the air-painting of fine, accurately placed lines.

PRECAUTIONS FOR THE AIR-BRUSH USER. Here are given some precautions to be observed in the correct use of the air brush for achieving the best results. These can be regarded as rules to be followed in all air-brush work.

Never begin air-brushing from the light area, but always from the dark.

Use an ink eraser for removing dark areas, and not a soft, greasy eraser.

Keep air-brush color stirred while it is in use.

Do not use color that has not been strained.

Keep color-mixing jars free from dirt and grit. Small, undissolved particles of color will prevent the proper passage of air in the air brush.

Keep surfaces to be air-brushed free from grease and dirt. Smudges will result when the air-brush spray is applied to dirty and greasy spots. Also keep all paint cloths free from grease and dirt.

Do not permit moisture to come in contact with the surface being air-brushed, and do not apply color to damp surfaces.

Keep the air brush moving in producing wash effects or smooth, blended tones. Use a rotating or fanning motion on large, flat surfaces.

CHAPTER III

CARE OF THE AIR BRUSH

CARE OF the air brush, at the outset, means cleanliness. The most important part of taking care of the air brush is to keep it clean. A dirty air brush, besides being a discredit to the artist who owns it or uses it, can not be expected to function properly, and its length of good service will be shortened considerably as a result.

CAREFUL CLEANING NECESSARY. If the air brush is not carefully cleaned while it is in use and after it is used, particles of ink or color on the needle or within the tip will act as a grinding abrasive, reducing the brush's capability of producing fine, sharp lines without feather edges. The valve and the washers must likewise be kept clean.

REMOVING COLOR. The air brush must be cleaned frequently while it is in use. If a water-soluble color is being used, clear, clean water should be forced through the air brush for a sufficient length of time to insure removal of all color from the barrel, needle, and other working parts. Air should be admitted into the brush for about five minutes after cleansing the brush with water.

Care should be taken that insoluble color, such as India ink, does not dry on the needle or other working parts. If a crust of dry color is allowed to form, the needle will have to be removed and scraped or be revolved in a bottle of fuller's earth. The fuller's earth should be dampened and tightly packed in a jar for this purpose.

Alcohol is a suitable cleaning fluid for alcohol-solvent colors, and turpentine should be used as a cleanser when oil colors have been used. An air brush cleaned with turpentine should be washed afterward with gasoline.

CARE OF THE NEEDLE. In using the needle-type air brush, great care should be taken in removing and cleaning the needle. The point of the needle should be protected to keep it from becoming bent, and the shaft should be kept straight, free from bending or distortion.

The cone tip, in which the point of the needle is articulated, should make a perfect union with the needle when the control button is free.

Damage to the point will affect the operation of the air brush. If the tip becomes bent, the delicate function of the air brush is impaired.

The air brush must not be dropped, and heavy objects must not be dropped on it or placed against it. If this care is not taken, the needle, tip, or other parts might be seriously damaged.

REPLACEMENTS. Tension springs in needle-type air brushes need to be replaced when the trigger becomes too "soft." For the cone-type air brush, several extra color parts, consisting of needle and cone, should be kept on hand. These parts should be in three different sizes —coarse, medium, and fine.

CLEANING COLOR CONTAINERS. Color containers, whether cups or jars, should be cleaned immediately after use; otherwise the color will cake, not only in the bottom of the color container, but also in the tube through which the color passes. Pipe cleaners can be used for removing color and dirt particles from the tube when necessary.

The air-brush hose and color cups should be kept in a box so that dust can not get into the working parts. The hose deteriorates with age and should be replaced every year. If it is not replaced, small particles of rubber from inside the hose will find their way into the working parts of the air brush.

CHAPTER IV

FRISKETS

AN IMPORTANT ADJUNCT in the use of the air brush is the frisket, or mask. A frisket as originally known was a light frame to hold a sheet of paper to the tympan in printing on a hand printing press. The name now also applies to a sheet stretched in a frame, with parts cut out to lay over an inked printing form, so that only certain parts shall be printed, as in color work. It is an adaptation of this latter form that is used in air-brush work.

THE AIR-BRUSH FRISKET. The air-brush frisket is applied as a mask or stencil over the design or illustration to be air-brushed to prevent certain parts of the design or illustration from being air-brushed with a certain color. It is cut either as a shape or as a stencil to govern the placement of the air-brush colors.

There are five principal kinds of friskets used in air-brush work. They are the photographer's frisket, the cement frisket, the partial frisket, the illustrator's frisket, and the fastened stencil. Each of these will be considered in turn.

MATERIALS REQUIRED. The principal materials required in the making of air-brush friskets are the frisket paper, frisket cement or rubber cement, a camel's-hair brush for applying the cement, and a stencil knife. Auxiliary materials include pins, thumb tacks, masking tape, rubber roller, plate glass, swabs, and benzine for diluting the rubber cement.

FRISKET PAPER. Frisket paper is especially adapted for the reproduction of designs and protection of the design when the air brush is used. It is fastened to the drawing or photograph with frisket cement or rubber cement. It is transparent and easy to cut.

Frisket paper is obtainable from art supply sources where air-brush equipment and colors are sold. Other kinds of paper are sometimes used for masking purposes, such as vellum, stencil board, or cardboard.

FRISKET CEMENT. Frisket cement is made especially for use with frisket paper. A high quality of rubber cement, such as used by artists, can also be used for attaching friskets to drawings or photographs. The cement is also procurable at sources of art supplies.

The rubber cement used should be of a quality that does not stain the surface to which it is applied. When the cement is required in a thinned consistency, as in the making of the cement frisket, it is diluted with benzine.

THE STENCIL KNIFE. The stencil knife should be of a type that affords flexibility in use—for cutting curved lines as well as straight ones, and for making intricate cuts as well as long, straight lines. The choice of a knife should also depend on its shape, and its keen-cutting qualities. The adjustable swivel knife with interchangeable blades is preferred by many artists, while others prefer the non-swivel type. The kind and shape of the knife handle also influence the artist in his choice.

THE PHOTOGRAPHER'S FRISKET. The procedure for making a photographer's frisket is as follows:

Attach the frisket paper to a sheet of illustration board with a few drops of cement applied to the corners. Then apply two coats of rubber cement to it. Strip the frisket paper from the board and lay it on the surface to be air-brushed. Press it carefully in place with the rubber roller and remove all wrinkles and air bubbles. The frisket is now ready for cutting with the stencil knife to remove the paper that covers areas of the design or illustration that are to be air-brushed with a given color.

THE CEMENT FRISKET. The cement frisket is made with a good grade of rubber cement diluted with benzine until it is of such a consistency that it can be brushed with a camel's-hair brush. Apply this solution to the surface of the drawing or photograph, spreading it uniformly without brush streaks. Allow it to dry until it will not be pulled up when a pencil point is touched to it. It is then ready to be cut with the stencil knife along the desired outlines in the same manner as frisket paper is cut. After the outlines have been cut, use a swab to remove the cement from the areas that are to be open for air-brushing.

THE PARTIAL FRISKET. The frisket known as the partial frisket is made by applying a good grade of rubber cement to outline only that part of the drawing to be air-brushed. Frisket paper or vellum paper, depending upon the transparency desired, is then applied over the drawing.   Then cut out the stencil where the cement has been applied to hold the edges of the stencil in place.   Be careful to remove the cement from the open areas with a swab, as any particle of the cement remaining on the working surface will spoil the appearance of the finished painting.

THE ILLUSTRATOR'S FRISKET.   To lay the illustrator's frisket apply the cement over the major part of the drawing and lay a heavy grade of vellum paper on the cement.   Smooth the vellum paper with the finger tips of both hands, working outward from the middle of the area, and remove all lumps beneath the paper.   A stiff card applied to the vellum can also be used.

THE FASTENED STENCIL.   The fastened stencil frisket is the ordinary stencil of vellum, stencil board, or cardboard, which has been cut to the desired shape.   This is attached to the working surface with pins, thumb tacks or masking tape, or it can be held in place with the hand.

PRECAUTIONS WHEN USING FRISKETS.   Do not use a mask or stencil where soft, blended effects are desired.

Mask an air-brushed drawing only for hard lines.

Do not ink a drawing after cutting into the outlines with a stencil knife, as a jagged line will result.

CHAPTER V

THE PRIMARY VALUE SCALE

THE MODERN METHOD of designating values of shade in art work is based upon a scale from light to dark, consisting of nine values. We term this as the primary value scale. Familiarity with this scale is of utmost importance, as most of the descriptions of light and shade in this text are based upon the nine values of the scale. Thorough knowledge of this scale is therefore the key to a complete and easy understanding of the values as designated and described in this book.

MAKING A PRIMARY VALUE SCALE. A piece of white illustration board 9 by 14 inches in size with a ½-inch border is ideal to use in making a primary value scale. Draw nine 1-inch squares on the card, spacing them ¼ inch apart in a vertical row, and number them from 1 to 9, beginning at the top square. Value 1 in this scale is white, value 9 is black, and value 5 is neutral, or medium gray. The numbering of this value scale is reversed from the usual practice of placing black at the top and white at the bottom.

APPLYING THE FRISKET. Outline the squares with rubber cement and apply a vellum-paper frisket over them. Square number 1 should be left covered with the frisket, since that square is to remain white, the same color as the cardboard. Cut the rest of the squares out of the frisket paper with the stencil knife and remove the excess rubber cement from the cardboard working surface within the open square areas.

AIR-BRUSHING THE SCALE. Air-brush square number 2, the second one from the top—the first open one—with a diluted India ink wash consisting of one part ink and three parts water. Next, air-brush the third square with value 3, which should be a little darker than value 2. Make each succeeding square darker than the preceding one, until value 9, or black, is reached. The darker values are obtained by re-airbrushing with a gray mixture which is value 3; however, the rendering of the scale can be hastened by darkening the mixture for

PRIMARY VALUE SCALE

1. white

2.

3. yellow

4. Red

5. Green

6. Blue

7. Blue Purple

8. Purple

9. Black

THE PRIMARY VALUE SCALE   Familiarity with this scale is of utmost importance, as most of the descriptions of light and shade in this text are based upon the nine values of the scale. In actual practice, value 1 is pure white and value 9 is solid black.

value 6, 7, and 8.   Value 9 or black can be painted out of the bottle of
ink with a paint brush.

LEARNING THE SCALE.   Practice repeatedly the making of the primary value scale until you have succeeded in developing uniform stages
of change from light to dark in the nine squares.   You should become
familiar enough with each of the values so that when one of them,
such as value 6, is mentioned, you will know that shade without having
to refer to the scale.   Until you have attained that familiarity, keep
your most uniform rendering of the scale before you for reference
when you practice using the air brush.

CHAPTER VI

AIR-BRUSHING DRILLS

THE THREE air-brushing drills described here will develop ability in three different phases of air painting. The first drill will develop ability to lay a smooth air-brushed wash. The second drill will develop ability to draw a spotless line with the air brush. The third drill will develop ability to air-brush color on a point or a small given area. This is sometimes called "pointing."

THE FIRST DRILL. The first drill is to air-brush three squares, each 4 by 4 inches in size and drawn with a pencil on white illustration

LINE DRILL. In air-brushing the lines, set the air-brush spray so it will produce the finest line possible and hold the tip of the air brush close to the working surface.

board. Mask these squares with a partial frisket made of vellum paper and fastened with rubber cement.

Lay a value 2 wash—one part India ink and three parts water—in the first square by holding the tip of the air brush about 8 inches from the surface and at a right angle to it, and by using an open adjustment for the color part or cone. Move the air brush across the surface horizontally, making a fanning motion with the wrist. Turn on the spray before it points into the square area, and turn it off after it leaves the area. This prevents spotting. Make the wash by working downward from the top of the square, using the horizontal fanning movement.

The second part of this drill is to lay a value 3 wash in the second square. Spray the square with the value 2 wash in the manner just described, and after the surface has dried thoroughly lay another wash over it, producing a value 3.

Follow the same procedure in air-brushing the third square, except that three value 2 washes are applied instead of two as in the second square. These three washes produce a value 4.

THE SECOND DRILL. The second drill is the producing of air-brushed horizontal, vertical, and diagonal lines free from dots, points, or spots. To do this, make a series of lightly drawn lines on illustration board with a medium hard pencil point. These lines should consist of horizontal lines 1 inch apart and about 8 inches long, vertical lines about 1 inch apart and about 8 inches long, and diagonal lines drawn on the 60-degree side of a 30-60-degree triangle. These diagonal lines should be about 1 inch apart and 10 inches long.

In the first exercise of air-brushing the lines, set the air-brush spray so it will produce the finest line possible and hold the tip of the air brush close to the working surface. After this exercise has been completed, repeat the air-brushing of the three sets of lines several times at different working distances from the surface of the illustration board. An ideal set of working distances for these repeated exercises is 3 inches, 5 inches, and 7 inches.

It is only by persistent repetition of these drills that you can gain sufficient control of the air brush to enable you to execute delicate details in illustration work.

THE THIRD DRILL. The third drill gives practice in coloring small areas uniformly. Draw four rows of circles on illustration board with

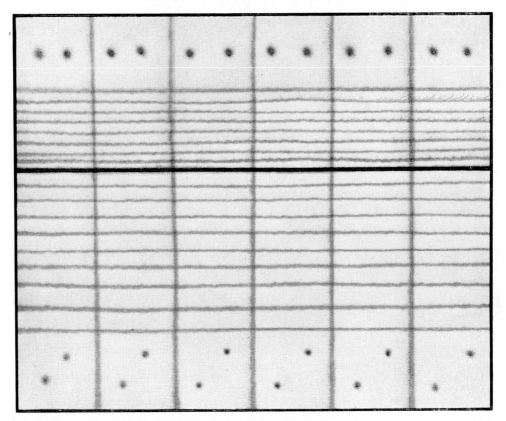

PRACTICE NECESSARY. Only persistent practice will enable the artist to manipulate his air brush to produce lines and points of uniform appearance.

a pencil, placing ten circles in each row. Make the circles in the first row 1 inch in diameter, those in the second row ½ inch in diameter, those in the third row ¼ inch in diameter, and those in the fourth row ⅛ inch in diameter. Color each of these circular areas uniformly without using a frisket, beginning with the largest areas and ending with the smallest.

OTHER DRILLS. Also practice other drills, such as those illustrated on pages 29 and 30, to add variety to the practice work. Proficiency in making air-brushed patterns similar to those pictured on page 30 will give you control of the air brush and enable you to execute delicate shading in fine illustrating. Make these squares about 4 inches square or larger and create the designs by air-brushing to the straight edge of a piece of cardboard held in position with the hand. Many unique and original designs can be created with this method, which is utilized a great deal in some forms of air-brush art. Variations can be supplied

DRILL SQUARES. Exercises such as these give the artist control of the air brush and enable him to execute delicate shading in illustration work.

by using masks with edges curved or in other shapes.

PERSISTENT PRACTICE NECESSARY. Only persistent practice of these drills will enable you to gain proficiency in the manipulating of the air brush. A thorough mastery of the fundamentals of air-brush art, such as these drills make possible, will make easy and pleasant the work to follow.

CHAPTER VII

USING COLOR

COLOR adds to the realism of illustrations and it gives life to art, whether it be applied with the air brush or any other medium of art expression. It appeals to the basic love of beauty that exists, either consciously or unconsciously, in all people. Color adds power and emphasis to an advertising layout. It brightens the illustration of a dull and uninteresting subject. An object that is colorless and drab in itself can be glorified by the addition of colored background or other atmospheric elements in color.

FORMS OF COLOR. All color can be classified according to use, as advancing or receding. The advancing colors are the warm hues, such as red, yellow, and yellow-red. The cool colors are receding. These cool colors include such hues as blue-purple, blue-green, and purple.

A portion of a drawing that is to be suppressed should be painted in a cool color, while a portion that is to stand out should be painted in warm colors. Illustrations of objects that are colorless can be forced toward the observer by simply applying a warm-colored background around them.

Warm colors have a tendency to tie together the multiple elements of a complex illustration. Cool-colored backgrounds tend to produce disassociation among the elements of a composition. For this reason, extreme care should be used when applying a cool-colored background to a drawing.

COLOR DEFINITION. All colors have three distinctions, namely, hue, value, and chroma. By hue is meant the color itself. By value is meant the amount of light present in a color. Value designates how light or how dark the hue is. By chroma is meant the strength or intensity of the color. Each color has its own strength, which is designated by units of chroma.

The values of color can be designated numerically according to its position relative to the gray value scale. Some colors are light in value,

yellow being value 3, while red is value 4. Other colors are dark in
value, blue-purple being value 7, while purple is value 8. This notation
is based on a scale with white as value 1 and black as value 9.

COLOR VALUES. The air-brush artist can prepare value scales of
each of the ten recognized basic colors, which are red, yellow-red,
yellow, yellow-green, green, blue-green, blue, blue-purple, purple, and
red-purple. In making up the value scales, a color may be lightened
in its value by the addition of white, and darkened by adding black.

The value scale can also be produced by increasing or decreasing
the amount of color applied to the working surface. This will give
values from the full intensity of the color to white. Darker values of
the color must be mixed before they are placed in the color cup.

Intensity scales can be made by mixing a color with its gray
equivalent in varying amounts. The intensity of a red may be reduced
by adding value 4 gray. The greater the amount of gray added for
the amount of red, the greater will be the degree of reduction in the
intensity of the red. Intensity scales can also be made by mixing a
color with it complement.

COLOR CONTRAST. Colors are at times strong by virtue of contrast.
Yellow in value 3 will appear strong next to a gray in value 8. Blue-
purple, in a dark value, appears intense next to yellow-green. Gray
backgrounds neutralize all colors placed upon them. They are to be
avoided wherever possible. Gray, however, can be used in connection
with a contrasting value of intense color. For example, light gray
cover stock can be used for an illustration in dark blue. Dark gray
stock can be used with an illustration in light orange or light yellow.

COLOR HARMONY. Color harmony falls into two classifications—
the harmony of contrasting colors and the harmony of related colors.
A painting in the different values of one color represents a related color
harmony. This is designated as a monochromatic harmony.

Where the colors in the harmony are unlike in hue, they present a
series of color harmonies known as the complementary harmonies, the
double complementary harmonies, and the split complementary harmonies. These are the contrasting color harmonies.

In the prevailing system of color notation such colors as red and
blue-green, yellow-green and purple, yellow-red and blue, yellow and
blue-purple, green and red-purple are complementary combinations.

Colors that are contrasting can be harmonized by the addition of a common color. In an air-brushed drawing in which there are areas of green, red, and blue, the values and chromas of those colors being such that there is a lack of color harmony, all three can be keyed by spraying a light, faint wash of red over the blue and green. They can likewise be keyed by spraying lightly with blue over the red and green.

When an air-brushed oil painting is varnished, the varnish will add a slight yellow cast to all the colors. These are then keyed by this common tint of yellow.

COLOR SCHEMES. Color schemes applied with the air brush should be kept as simple as possible as far as the number of hues is concerned, whether the drawing is for display or for reproduction. Simplicity in color schemes insures generally the application of two basic laws of color in design—first, the repetition of each color in different parts of the layout that will produce beauty or harmony, and second, the contrast of the one color selected for the dominant area. This will likewise produce color emphasis.

All colors should be considered from the standpoint of (1) harmony, (2) balance, and (3) emphasis or dominance. Over-repetition of color is dangerous, as it is apt to produce monotony. The repetition of a color three times is an ideal plan to use in design. In a poster layout, color harmony can be produced by repeating the color at regular intervals in the poster area. Nature employs this device in many flowering plants.

COLOR AND LIGHT. In preparing air-brushed designs for store fronts and large-scale displays, the artist should consider the ability of color to reflect or absorb light, as the case might be. This is especially noticeable in display window interiors.

Light colors reflect light; dark colors absorb it. Display windows should be designed in the colors that will illuminate the merchandise. If the art work is to be under strong illumination or glare, colors selected should be those that will absorb light to offset the glare.

EFFECTS OF COLORS. A colored background will influence the colors of the elements placed against them. A red background with an extremely dark green object placed against it will cause the intensity of the green to be lessened or partially neutralized.

Light colors, whether warm or cool, have a tendency to exaggerate the size of the area to which they are applied. This tendency is slightly greater in light warm colors than in light cool colors.

Dark colors seem to decrease the sizes of the areas to which they are applied. This is more apparent in cool colors than in the low-value warm hues. An area painted black adjoining an area painted in color will have two effects. One is to cause the color area to appear slightly smaller and the other is to cause the value of the color in the color area to be diminished.

Color is used in advertising art and some other forms of art for the effect it will produce upon the individual who observes the art work containing the color. Red, for example, suggests the physical state of heat, while blue suggests coolness. Certain colors likewise express certain emotions. Red expresses anger, purple expresses dignity, brown expresses cheerfulness and happiness, and yellow expresses joy.

COLOR FATIGUE. Color fatigue is one of the most important factors to be prevented and overcome in the design of illustrations and advertising layouts. Warm colors set up more eye fatigue than cool colors. Extremely large areas of a color also increase the fatigue of the eyes. The observer will unconsciously turn away from an area that produces an unnecessary amount of color fatigue.

Color monotony must be avoided, as this also produces color fatigue. Color monotony is generally caused by a spotted type of layout in which the color appears at spaced intervals. Monotony is also caused by the over-repetition of color and the over-application of color to areas.

COLOR MEDIUMS. In his use of color, the air-brush artist has a large range and variety of color mediums from which to select. Colors can be classified according to physical properties as waterproof, permanent, or temporary.

Colored inks and Japanese book colors are ideal for air-brush use, especially in extremely sensitive air brushes. Pigment colors can be used if the pigment is finely ground. Coarsely ground water colors should be avoided, as they tend to dry around the needle and consequently clog the air brush. A small particle of color is sufficient to cause clogging.

Oil colors should be used only in the display type of air brush, and the instrument should be constantly cleaned with gasoline when oil colors are used. The best grade of studio tube oil colors should be selected and thinned with drying oil and medicinal turpentine. Oil colors can be used for outdoor signs and displays if the studio tube colors are used. Alcohol solvent waterproof colors can also be used for outdoor work.

THE COLORS TO USE. The following is an outline of the kinds of colors to use in the air brush for the various purposes named:

Architectural renderings—pan colors, tube water colors, Japanese book colors, colored inks.

Monument renderings—Japanese book colors, colored inks, tube water colors.

Portraits—finely ground show-card colors, opaque tube water colors, moist water colors, bottle air-brush colors, alcohol solvent colors.

Full-color illustrating—colored inks, tube water colors, pan colors, bottle air-brush colors, and dry colors.

Displays and display cards—moist water colors, dry colors, finely ground show-card colors.

Photo retouching—retouch colors.

Fashion drawings—tube water colors, colored inks, dye colors.

Murals—high-grade and finely ground studio tube oil colors.

PART II

FORM REPRESENTATION

CHAPTER VIII

THE CYLINDER AND CONE

ONCE YOU HAVE familiarized yourself with the working of the air brush and have had practice in the making of friskets and the using of the air brush in air-brush drills and in producing primary value scales so that you can handle the instrument and control it with confidence, you are ready to enlarge your practice by making air-brushed paintings of form representations in light and shade.

SIMPLE FORMS. First to be considered is the representation of simple forms in light and shade, or black and white. These simple forms are the basic geometric solids, such as the cylinder, cone, cube, sphere, prism, and the irregular solids.

FORM REPRESENTATION. Every conceivable object can be analyzed to take the basic shape of one or more of the simple geometric forms. An understanding of the fundamentals in shading each of these simple forms therefore enables you to cope with the problem of shading any object in illustration.

In any form of study, a good groundwork knowledge of fundamentals makes easy the more complex work to come. With a carefully laid groundwork in these fundamentals of form representation, you should therefore have little difficulty in making rapid progress in your later work.

THE CYLINDER. The forms of many objects are represented by the cylinder in one position or another. The drawing that shows conventional illumination of a smooth, upright cylinder has the line of highlight about half way between the left edge and the vertical center line, while the line of maximum shade is present slightly in from and parallel to the right edge.

The gradation of values from the left edge to the line of highlight

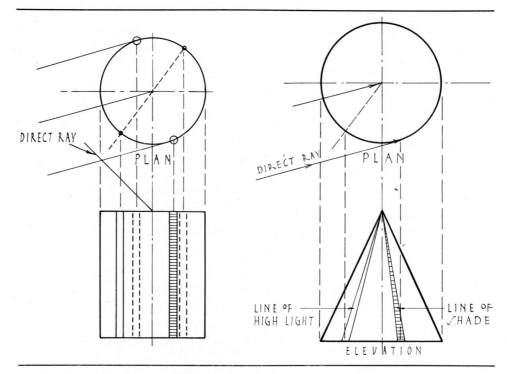

THE CYLINDER AND CONE. Plan views of the cylinder (left) and cone (right) under conventional illumination.

across the average upright cylinder composed of a substance that readily reflects the light is from value 3 to value 1. Value 1 is the highlight, and from this highlight to the line of maximum shade is a range of values from 2 through 8 to value 9. From the line of maximum shade to the right is a gradation of value 9 to 8, and then value 7 to the right edge. This is based on using value 1 as white and value 9 as black.

SKETCHING THE CYLINDER. The first step in making an airbrushed painting of the cylinder is to draw an outline sketch of the cylinder form. Make this sketch on a good grade of illustration board that is free from grease stains and pencil smudges. When the sketch is properly drawn, the values designated in the preceding paragraph should be marked very lightly on the drawing, and the line of highlight and the line of maximum shade should be accurately located on the shape.

MAKING THE FRISKET. Apply frisket cement to the outline of the drawing, and over the cement lay a sheet of transparent vellum paper.

Lay this carefully and roll it down to insure its close adhesion to the working surface. Cut out the vellum paper over the top of the sketched cylinder and wipe the revealed portion of the working surface with a clean cloth or swab to remove all the cement.

AIR-BRUSHING THE TOP. Begin applying the color with the air brush to the cut-out portion of the drawing, using a good grade of air-brush water-color black diluted so that it flows easily through the air brush. In making the air-brushed shading on the top of the cylinder, hold the tip of the air brush about 2 inches from the working surface and use a rotating motion. Concentrate the spray somewhat on the two ends of the ellipse representing the top of the cylinder. The edge of this ellipse that is away from the observer should be darker

THE CYLINDER. Every conceivable object can be analyzed to take the basic shape of one or more of the simple geometric forms. The forms of many of these objects are represented by the cylinder in one position or another. This is the air-brushed cylinder under conventional illumination.

than the forward edge. Cover the air-brushed surface, when it is dry, with a mask of cardboard or paper.

AIR-BRUSHING THE SIDE. Make a frisket for air-brushing the rest of the cylinder form by cutting through the vellum paper around the outline of the form. Remove the cut-out portion and wipe the cement from the opening on the working surface as before.

Begin with the line of maximum shade in air-brushing this portion of the illustration, using an up-and-down motion, and gradually work toward the right edge to produce values 8 and 7. Then, beginning at the left edge, apply values 3 and 2 with the same up-and-down motion. Air-brushing of the intermediate values from 2 to 9 completes the painting.

HOW SURFACES AFFECT VALUE RANGE. A cylinder with a rough surface does not reflect light so readily as one with a smooth texture and therefore the value range on the rough surface is not so great. Another factor that affects the value range is the amount of contrast in the actual color of the object. Dark colors tend to absorb light, so that the representation in light and shade of a smooth-surfaced cylinder that is actually dark red will show a value range from 4 to 9. If the texture of the dark red cylinder is rough, then the gradation of values is further reduced.

THE CONE. The second form representation to be studied is the cone—a form that represents many parts of the human body. Such muscles as the biceps and triceps in the arm are conical in shape.

The illustration of the cone to be studied presents a triangular line of highlight at the left, extending from the apex to the base. This line intersects the base about half way between the vertical center line and the left edge. A triangular-shaped line of maximum shade is on the right side. This shade area extends from the apex to the base, the base intersection being the point of tangency of the conventional light ray. This ray makes an angle of 15 degrees with the picture plane, which will show as a 15-degree angle with the horizontal center line through the base circle of the cone.

From the line of highlight to the outermost left edge of the cone illustration are values 2 and 3. Extending from the highlight to the line of maximum shade the gradation of values is from value 2 through 8. Values 8 and 7 are in the area between the line of maximum shade, which is value 9, and the extreme right edge.

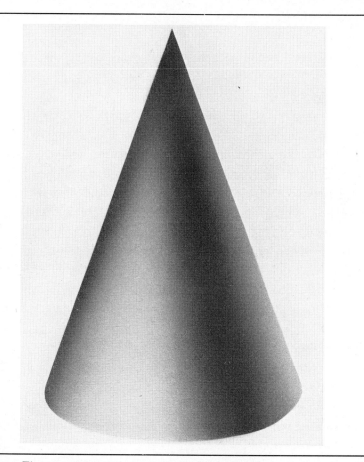

THE CONE. The second form representation to be studied is the cone—a form that represents many parts of the human body.

AIR-BRUSHING THE CONE. Make an outline sketch of the cone form and indicate thereon the values as just designated. Apply the frisket to the drawing, using frisket cement and vellum paper, the same as when air-brushing the cylinder. If the base of the cone is not shown in the drawing, cut out the entire area of the cone with the stencil knife.

Begin shading at the line of maximum shade, gradually lightening the shade toward the line of highlight and toward the extreme right. Hold the air brush about 2 inches from the working surface and move it up and down in the direction of the shape of the cone.

Differences in the value ranges according to the texture and actual color of the conical object are the same as those already described for the cylinder.

CHAPTER IX

THE CUBE, SPHERE, AND PRISM

CONTINUING the descriptions of form representation with the air brush, this chapter presents studies of three more solids—the cube, sphere, and prism. These, like the cylinder and the cone, as well as the other solids still to be considered, will be found representative of many forms used in illustration work with the air brush. In making illustrations of these solids, the procedure of sketching the shape and applying the frisket is the same as described in the preceding chapter.

THE CUBE. The cube is a six-sided solid consisting of flat surfaces, each at a right angle to each of the surfaces at its four adjacent sides. It is a shape that by simple rotation can be made to assume an infinite number of positions, each of which has its own value range with reference to the source of illumination upon it. All the values, however, that are to be found on the cube's surfaces are based upon four simple rules of shading.

RULES OF SHADING. The first of these four rules of shading is that the shading of a surface which is normal, or parallel to the picture plane, is constant in value. This surface is generally value 1, or white, if the illumination is of strong intensity.

The second rule is that when a surface which is normal, or parallel to the picture plane, is in shade, the shade is constant in value. This constant value approaches 9, or black, as the extreme, and it is dependent upon the amount of illumination.

The third rule is that the portion of a flat upright surface in perspective nearest the observer is lightest, and the area at the greatest distance from the observer is darkest in value. In this case, the light-and-shade value range on a flat surface in perspective is from a light gray to a dark tone, depending upon the size of the surface and the intensity of the illumination cast upon it. A horizontal surface in perspective should have a value range from a light foreground to a dark background.

The fourth rule is that when in shade the portion of a flat surface

THE CUBE. The cube is a shape that by simple rotation can be made to assume an infinite number of positions, each of which has its own value range with reference to the source of illumination upon it.

in perspective nearest the observer is darkest and the portion at greatest distance from the observer is lightest. This is opposite to the shading of the flat surface in illumination. The actual value range from dark to light on the surface will vary according to the position.

LIGHT AND SHADE. When analyzing the cube from the standpoint of light and shade, constantly bear in mind the effect of the size of the cube upon the value range. In order to apply the four rules of shading, study carefully the position of the cube to determine just what part of the surface is nearest and what parts are at greatest distance from the observer.

THE CUBE IN SIMPLE PERSPECTIVE. When a cube is resting on a table plane and is turned in a perspective position, the nearest corner of the top shows a dead light, or white. The gradation increases in darkness until value 4 or 5 is reached on the portion of the surface farthest from the observer.

On the illuminated side, the range is from almost value 2 to value 5, depending upon the actual size of the cube. On the shaded side, the darkest area is that portion nearest the observer.

THE CUBE ON EDGE. When the cube is in illumination and is turned so that it rests on an edge in such a way that it has three visible surfaces, all in perspective, the top surface that is visible is illuminated, while the other two visible surfaces are in shade. It is interesting to note, when the cube is in this position, that one side surface in shade is darkest from the top downward, while the other side surface in shade is darkest from the top and forward edge outward.

THE CUBE IN PARALLEL PERSPECTIVE. When the cube is drawn in parallel perspective, one surface is square in construction, and it automatically becomes, according to the rules of shading, a normal surface that is constant in value, usually with a flat tone of light value if the surface is relatively small. The perspective flat surface at the top is lightest nearest the observer and darkest away from the observer. The square or normal surface, however, should be treated with some sort of tracery of light and shade, which is assumed by the artist. This tracery is generally provided by reflection of a light or shade from other objects supposed to be in the vicinity of the cube.

THE SPHERICAL SURFACE. The spherical surface is one that occurs in many objects. It is to be found especially in machine parts. In

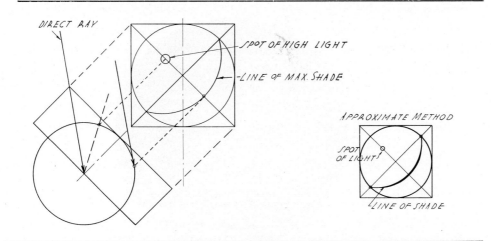

THE SPHERICAL SURFACE. In arriving at the values on a spherical surface, first inclose the solid in a cube. This inscribed sphere presents in elevation the appearance of a circle within a square.

arriving at the values on a spherical surface, first inclose the solid in a cube. This inscribed sphere presents in elevation the appearance of a circle within a square.

LOCATING THE HIGHLIGHT. A projected view is then taken across the sphere-inclosing cube so that its surface presents an angle of 45 degrees to the observer. A conventional light ray is drawn through the center of the sphere and through the upper left corner of the cube in this position. The angle of this line with the vertical center line is bisected, and this bisecting line is projected through the solid to locate the spot of highlight on the lower side. The point of intersection of the bisector with the circle is projected to the body diagonal to form the spot of highlight.

THE LINE OF MAXIMUM SHADE. A tangent to the circle parallel to the original ray to the center of the sphere locates the point of shade on the projected view. Through this point, draw a line parallel to the line of centers to the front view until it intersects the body diagonal. This intersection, when joined to the two intersection points of the sphere with the other body diagonal, gives three points, which when joined describe the curve of the line of maximum shade.

SHADING THE SPHERE. The line of maximum shade on the sphere should be air-brushed in value 9, or black. From this line to the lower side of the sphere, the shade lightens slightly through values 8 and 7.

SHADING THE SPHERE. The line of maximum shade on the sphere should be air-brushed in value 9, or black. From this line to the lower side of the sphere, the shade lightens slightly through values 8 and 7. The spherical surface is one that occurs in many objects. It is to be found especially in machine parts.

From that line to the spot of highlight, the values lighten until value 1 is reached. The values on the top left area are light, usually 3 or 4. There is a tendency, in air-brushing the sphere, to form ring-like value bands around the spot of highlight to the line of maximum shade.

THE PRISM. The prism is a solid figure with two ends as similar, equal, and parallel rectilineal figures usually triangular in shape, and with sides as parallelograms. It is another solid whose form can be utilized in the making of air-brushed representations of many objects that the air-brush artist is called upon to reproduce. Sometimes the form is that of the regular-shaped prism, while at other times it is that of extreme shapes, such as the wedge. The theory of shading the regular-shaped prism should be mastered first.

THE PRISM. The prism is another solid whose form can be utilized in the making of air-brushed representations of many objects that the air-brush artist is called upon to reproduce.

LIGHT VALUES ON THE PRISM. The light values on a prism vary according to its position. If it is placed with a flat surface toward the observer, the shading on this surface is reduced to value 1, or white. When this surface is presented, the artist must resort to the use of real or reflected lights.

If, on the other hand, the prism is turned at a slight angle, it becomes a perspective flat surface in illumination or shade, depending upon the angle of the light rays striking it. If it is turned still more, it shows two surfaces, one of which is in illumination and one of which is in shade. These two perspective flat surfaces have a slight difference in value range unless their extremities are the same projected distance from the picture plane passed through the apex of the prism. For example, if the prism is turned so that one of the sides is at a small angle to the picture plane while the other is at a sharp angle, there is a greater value range on the sharp-angle side than on the small-angle side.

CHAPTER X

MANY-SIDED SOLIDS ·

FORMS REPRESENTED by many-sided solids are being used to a surprising extent in modern illustrating and designing. They are found in package designs, carton shapes, electric signs, window displays, tables, perfume bottles, cosmetic containers, and in many other objects. These shapes are also common in mechanical subjects, such as machine parts.

THE HEXAHEDRON. The hexahedron, a solid figure with six faces, is generally found in two positions. One position shows one surface parallel to the observer, and the other shows each surface at an angle to the observer. The first-named position can be considered as the normal one.

THE NORMAL POSITION. When the hexahedron is in the position showing one surface parallel to the observer, the light on that surface is constant and equal to value 1 under conventional illumination. The left perspective surface is in illumination with the light concentrated on the forward edge and with the shade on the portion at the far edge. This shade, however, seldom exceeds value 5, the range being from value 1 to value 5 for the entire surface. The perspective surface at the right in this view is in shade. Its nearest portion is dark, usually a value 9, and it is lightened toward the far portion to a value 6. The top, if shown, presents a range of from value 1 to 4 from front to rear.

The flat surface parallel to the observer is sometimes treated with a real or assumed tracery of shade to give the entire solid a realistic appearance. This tracery is usually concentrated as a shade at the top or bottom of the surface, but not at the middle. The value range should be confined from value 1 to value 6 or less.

THE ANGLE POSITION. The second or angle position of the hexahedron shows each surface at an angle to the observer. It presents two perspective surfaces, one in illumination, and one in shade. The illuminated surface has a gradation of from value 1 to value 5, while the surface in shade has a range of from value 9 to value 6 or 7. The

THE HEXAHEDRON. This is the hexahedron in normal position with one surface parallel to the observer. The light on that surface is constant and equal to value 1 under conventional illumination. The surface is sometimes treated with a real or assumed tracery of shade to give the entire solid a realistic appearance.

top surface, if exposed, shows a range of from value 1 to value 4 when the solid is slightly below eye level. The far area is darkened more as the shape is dropped below eye level.

THE OCTAHEDRON. The octahedron, a solid figure contained by eight plane faces, is a solid that can be placed with one surface parallel to the observer and the rest in perspective to the observer, or it can be turned so that each surface is at an angle to the observer. It has in a general way the same pattern of light and shade as the hexahedron, with two exceptions. First, because of the greater number of surfaces, the value range on each surface is less. Also, because of the change in the angle of each surface, the values themselves will be changed.

THE NORMAL POSITION. When the octahedron is in what can be called the normal position, with one surface parallel to the observer, only three surfaces are shown. The shading is the same as for the hexahedron in normal position. The tracery on the flat surface should be modified, however, because of the narrow width. The value range on the left surface, which is illuminated, is from value 1 to value 4,

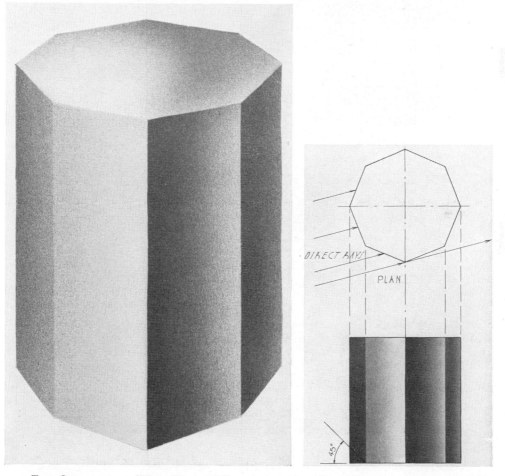

THE OCTAHEDRON. When the octahedron is turned so that four surfaces are presented to the observer, two of them are in illumination and two in shade if the vertical center line coincides with the middle element line.

and on the right surface, which is shaded, from value 8 to value 5.

THE ANGLE POSITION. When the octahedron is turned so that four surfaces are presented to the observer, two of them are in illumination and two in shade if the vertical center line coincides with the middle element line. In this position, the foreshortened width of the left surface coincides with that of the right surface. The flat angle of the first surface to the left of the middle line has a range from white, or value 1, to a very light value at the edge. The change of

A MANY-SIDED SOLID. Forms represented by many-sided solids are being used to a surprising extent in modern illustrating and designing. They are found in package designs, carton shapes, electric signs, window displays, tables, perfume bottles, cosmetic containers, and in many other objects. They are also common in mechanical subjects, such as machine parts.

angle causes the extreme left surface to have a middle tone which is increased in value to a dark tone at the edge. On the right side, the first surface from the middle is the darker. This value diminishes toward the edge of the plane. The outermost shaded surface, with its increased angle, is lighter in value. The peculiar thing about the octahedron in this position is that a line of white occurs in the middle next to a region of dark.

SURFACES AFFECT VALUE RANGE. The value ranges on the surfaces of the hexahedron and the octahedron vary according to the textures of the surfaces and according to the surface size, as well as the intensity of the illumination. As a general rule, the rougher the surface of each plane, the less change in value there is on it. As the texture is roughened, its ability to reflect light is lessened, causing the reduction of value contrast.

CHAPTER XI

INDENTED SURFACES

THE AIR-PAINTING of illustrations of indented surfaces is an interesting form of study and one that will prove to be of considerable value in the course of an air-brush artist's regular work. Ample practice should therefore be devoted to the air-painting of various forms of indented surfaces.

THE V-SHAPED INDENTATION. When the indented surface is turned so that its far end is to the left, the exposed part of the indentation shows the darkest values at the bottom of the indentation, and the lightest values are toward the top. The same surface turned so that its far end is to the right shows a line of shade about one-third of the way up from the bottom of the V, decreasing to lighter values at the bottom.

VALUES UNDER DIRECT LIGHT. When the illumination is directly over the indented surface, the upper parts of the surface are light. These planes darken in value toward the bottom of the indentation.

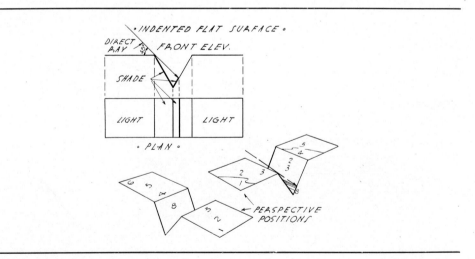

INDENTED SURFACES. Plan view (above) and perspective views of V-shaped indented surfaces in two positions. The numbers indicate values of light and shade according to the primary value scale.

54

THE CURVED INDENTATION. In the shading of the curved indentation, a line of shade is shown when the length of the horizontal plane
is turned to the left toward the light. The values diminish in both
directions from this line in the exposed part of the curved area. When
the length of the surface is turned to the right, a line of light is seen
on the exposed curved portion. This light becomes darker toward the
top horizontal plane, and below it the value changes abruptly from
light to a line of maximum shade caused by the light being obstructed
from the curved surface.

THE V-SHAPED INDENTATION. These V-shaped indentations are air-brushed in the two
perspective positions shown in the preceding sketches.

PART III

ADVERTISING DISPLAYS

CHAPTER XII

LETTERING WITH THE AIR BRUSH

IN LETTERING with the air brush for reproduction purposes as well as for various forms of display advertising, you can surprise yourself with the novel and interesting effects it is possible to produce with comparatively little practice and effort if you have a good fundamental knowledge of lettering art.   One air-brush artist aptly described these effects when he said that he could make his air brush "talk" for him when he used it to make unusual letter forms for special treatments, such as icicles for cold, flames for heat, ribbon letters, rope letters, simulated neon sign letters, and many others.

MAKING AIR-BRUSHED LETTERING.   Air-brushed letters can be formed in several ways—by simply drawing them and air-brushing free-hand to the drawing outline; by cutting and air-brushing a stencil for the lettering; by forming the letters with masking tape; by using stock stencil letters; by spraying around letter forms, or by holding a piece of cardboard against the working surface, spraying to its edge, and then moving the cardboard to a new position.

A desirable method of lettering with the air brush is with the use of the cut-out stencil.   A variety of effects can be achieved by simply leaving the centers white or by concentrating the spray in the upper or the lower portion of the stencil.   When masking tape is used, the letters can be quickly formed if they are of the block style.   It is not advisable to use this method for extremely fancy lettering.

CAST SHADOW LETTERS.   Letter shadows made with the air brush are a means of emphasizing a word or line of words.   These shadows can be classified as the cast shadow, the dropped shadow, the table shadow, the vertical cast shadow, the inclined cast shadow, and the perspective shadow.

NORMAL CAST SHADOWS. One method of procedure in air-brushing normal cast shadow letters is as follows:

Construct the letters with lettering brush or pen and draw a pencil outline of the letter shadows. Over this drawing, fasten a sheet of transparent vellum and cut out the shadows with the stencil knife. Place the shadow color, which can be a contrasting color to the letters themselves, in the air-brush cup. Hold the air brush with its tip about 3 inches from the working surface. Move the air brush in the direction of the letter shadow, concentrating the spray next to the original letter so that the shadow appears to fade away from it.

A second method of producing a cast shadow is to cut a stencil for the lettering and spray through this to produce the original letters. A stencil is then cut for the shadows, which are air-brushed as just described.

A third method is to make the letters with brush or pen and then apply the cast shadow by using a small piece of cardboard for a mask. Air-brushing to the edge of the card forms the straight lines of the shadow. The card can be held in the hand and moved as the work proceeds.

NORMAL CAST SHADOWS. There are three methods of procedure in air-brushing normal cast shadow letters.

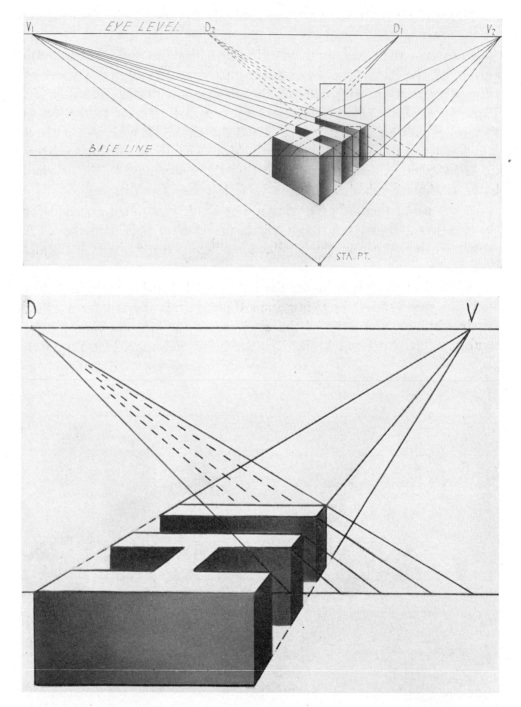

In Perspective. These air-brushed cast shadow letters are constructed in perspective.

INCLINED CAST SHADOWS. Using the inclined cast shadow made with the air brush is another way to give emphasis to key words of advertising copy. The amount of force that this shadow has depends upon the angle of shadow with reference to the original letter. If this angle is sharp enough, the lettering can be read twice.

To construct the inclined cast shadow, the letter forms should be carefully made. For display lettering the forms should be one-stroked between the capital line and the base line. The capital line is dropped below its original position for the inclined cast shadow. Direct

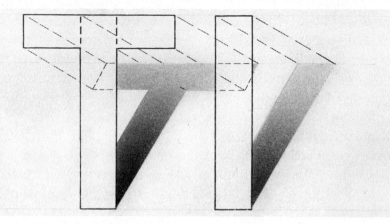

INCLINED CAST SHADOWS. Using the inclined cast shadow is another way to give emphasis to key words of advertising copy. If the angle of shadow is sharp enough, the lettering can be read twice.

light rays are drawn across the structural points of the letter forms and the intersection of these rays is taken with the dropped capital line. These points of intersection are then joined to the external points of the letter that touch the base line.

In drawing the inclined cast shadow of the letter "A," a vertical center line is drawn through the letter and the shadow of this center line is plotted by drawing a direct ray through the apex of the letter to the dropped capital line. This point of intersection is joined with the intersection of the original center line with the base line. The point of intersection of the inclined center line with the dropped capital line is connected with the two intersection points of the legs of the "A" and the base line. This forms the outside lines of the inclined cast shadow "A."

To produce leg thickness, parallel lines to the shadow lines are drawn through the innermost intersections of the legs of the "A" with the base line. To form the bar of the "A," direct rays are drawn through the structural points of the bar on the left leg of the "A" until they intersect the corresponding leg of the shadow letter. Horizontal lines are drawn through these points, forming the shadow bar. Other inclined letters, such as the V, W, X, and Y, can be constructed in a like manner.

To construct the inclined cast shadow of the rounded letters, such as O, C, and G, a center line is first drawn through the original letter and the inclined cast shadow center line is constructed from it. A number of points are then taken on the curve, and through these points 45-degree direct rays are drawn. The original point is projected to the base line. A line parallel to the inclined center line (or shadow center line) is drawn through this point. The intersection of the 45-degree ray line with this parallel line locates the point on the shadow letter.

All points on the curve can be plotted in a like manner. If the letter has extreme thickness, plot the outside curve first and the inside curve second. All rounded letters can be plotted by this procedure.

TABLE SHADOWS. The table shadow is one that is cast in front of

TABLE SHADOWS. The table shadow is one that is cast in front of the letter. It gives the effect of the letter standing on a base and casting a shadow on the base.

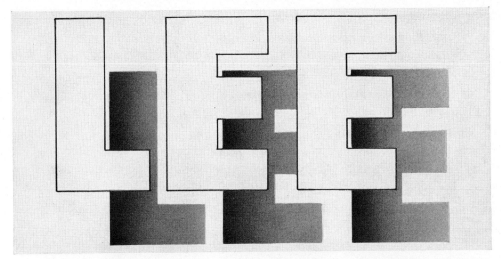

DROPPED SHADOWS   There are several ways of producing dropped shadows with the air brush.   The result gives an effect appropriate to numerous applications in lettering art.

the letter. It gives the effect of the letter standing on a base and casting a shadow on the base.

The procedure for executing the letters and table shadow with the air brush is first to lay out the lettering and shadow on vellum paper. The stencil of both lettering and shadow can be cut at one time. Apply this with cement over the surface that is to receive the lettering. Lay a piece of cardboard over the shadow forms while spraying the original letters. After this lettering is dry, place the cardboard mask over it while spraying the shadow. It is best to keep the shadow forms light in value to insure giving the proper emphasis to the letters from which the shadow forms are cast.

DROPPED SHADOWS. There are several ways of producing dropped shadows with the air brush. Two of them will be considered here. Whatever the exact method of procedure might be, the result gives an interesting effect appropriate to numerous applications in lettering art.

If the lettering is drawn on the surface to be air-brushed, vellum paper is laid over the surface and a tracing is made. The lettering on the tracing is then cut out to form a stencil. This stencil is placed over the surface and moved down until it is the desired distance from the original letters. The pattern is then sprayed. A color should be used that is in contrast to the color of the original letters, and the tip of the air brush should be held 2 inches from the surface of the work. The spray should be directed around the edge of the stencil. Multiple dropped shadows can be produced by repeatedly moving the stencil down and spraying with the desired color or colors.

Another way of producing the dropped shadow is simply to lay off the letters on vellum paper and then cut them out to form the stencil. This stencil is first used to produce the letters, and then to produce the shadow.

EXPRESSIVE LETTER FORMS. Letters that appear to be burning can

EXPRESSIVE LETTER FORMS. In lettering with the air brush for reproduction purposes as well as for various forms of display advertising, you can surprise yourself with the novel and

be atomized through a stencil in black, and the upper portions of them can be made red. Heat waves can be shown ascending above the letters by setting the air brush to a line adjustment and atomizing red in wavy lines above the lettering.

An effect of cold, shivering lettering can be produced by cutting a wavy outlined stencil of the lettering, and atomizing with blue-green,

interesting effects it is possible to produce with comparatively little practice and effort if you have a good fundamental knowledge of lettering art.

blue-gray, and white to represent coldness. On such lettering, the white blended into the letter color will give the effect of snow. Icicles can be drawn on the letters and air-brushed in blue-gray and white.

Rustic lettering effects can be made with the air brush by spraying the solid color first, and then embellishing the letters with the aid of a movable cardboard mask. The letters can be made to appear as if formed from woody vines or bent tree branches. In shading the solid color the method of shading the cylinder should be followed to give the effect of a curved surface.

Normal Gothic letters can be constructed with irregular wedge-shaped shadows to produce novel effects. Attractive script lettering can also be constructed so that it appears to be made of a piece of ribbon or strip of bent metal.

Lettering can be treated so that it appears to be cut out of marble. The texture of the marble is produced by streaking rubber cement across the face of the lettering and air-brushing over it. The cement is removed after the color has dried. This can be repeated several times to produce variety in effect.

Lettering that represents smoke or sky writing can be easily made free-hand with the air brush. It should be first stroked in the width desired, and then intensified by additional air-brushing in the middle of each letter stroke with the air brush set at a fine line adjustment.

Novelty lettering can be made by bending the letters backward in a curve and applying the color with the air brush according to the theory of shading the cylinder. Another novelty effect is created by simply spraying around various-sized can tops that are shifted about over the surface of the lettering. A variation of this is to use silhouettes of animals or other forms.

CHAPTER XIII

AIR-BRUSHED DISPLAYS

ADVERTISING DISPLAYS that are produced either wholly or partially with the air brush have advantages that distinguish them from ordinary displays, provided, of course, that the air-brushed displays are properly executed.

ADVANTAGES OF AIR-BRUSHING. The air-brushed display has many advantages. It can be made as modern looking and as colorful as the advertiser desires. Air-brushing permits the use of attractively blended color effects that are otherwise impossible to attain. Air-brushed work can be harmoniously combined with hand lettering and design, and with screen-process methods of reproduction.

Air brushing is ideal for producing small quantities of displays, all of the same design and treatment. The use of the same stencil for all the display pieces makes this possible. The stencil can be kept for future use, too, should it be likely that additional quantities of the same display will be required at another time.

Rapid execution of illustrations is made possible with the air brush for displays that must be quickly made and yet have the added distinction and advertising value that only a suitable illustration can give.

AIR-BRUSHED DISPLAY CARDS. There are numerous methods in which air-brushed display cards can be produced. Some of these methods are followed because of the kind of display cards being produced, some are used because of materials with which the artist works, and others are used because of lack of knowledge regarding better methods.

PREPARING THE CARD. There are six steps in this procedure for the making of an air-brushed display card. The first step is the making of the rough thumb-nail sketch. The second step is the making of the actual layout in desired size on the stencil paper. The third step is the cutting of the stencil or stencils, followed by the applying of the stencil to the display-card surface with masking tape or frisket cement, pins or thumb tacks. The fifth step is the applying of the color with the

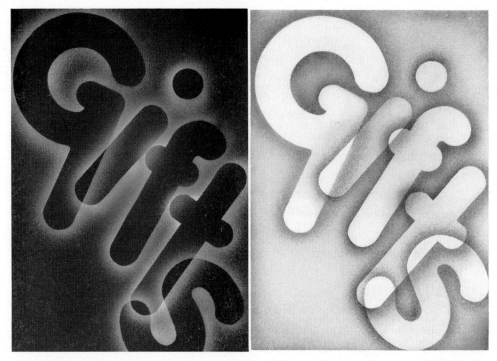

Two Treatments. How two different display treatments can be achieved—one in silhouette, the other in highlight.

air brush, and last is the removal of the stencil and the touching-up of the card by hand, if this is found necessary.

APPLYING THE COLOR.   The air brush can be of a type that permits the application of any good grade of show-card color without clogging. It should not be too sensitive or it will have a tendency to clog.

In applying the color, the lettering on the display card can be given a uniform tone, or the color can be concentrated on one side of each letter and blended out to the other side.   To give yet another effect, the color can be applied to only the edges of the letters, giving them a rounded appearance, with the color of the card surface showing through in the letter strokes.   These different methods of air-painting the letters through the stencil can be employed in the different blocks of lettering on the same card to make each portion stand out.   Good taste, however, must govern the extent of this practice.

FOR DECORATIVE EFFECTS.   When decorative borders or other effects are desired on the display card, make the stencil for the decorative design only, which can be applied with the air brush.   The lettering can then be done by hand with lettering pens or brushes.

To produce a completely air-brushed display card with a decorative design, make separate stencils for the design and lettering, and air-brush the design with one color and the lettering with another. The result is a two-color display card of a kind adaptable to the advertising of a variety of items. This procedure can of course be elaborated to include more colors in both the design and the lettering.

SEASONAL DISPLAY CARDS. Effective display cards of seasonal nature can be air-brushed on special kinds or patterns of cardboard stock. Using a brown background, for example, a design consisting of geese flying across the face of the full moon lends itself to a treatment of spraying around the stencils for the design, instead of through them, with a color such as white or yellow. Other seasonal subjects, such as autumn leaves, snow-covered evergreen trees, and candles, can be prepared by using light yellow color on a brown background.

Air-brushed creations in two or more colors can be effectively prepared by using dark blue or black air-brushed effects on the brown background for the subdued part of the design and white or yellow for the principal parts. Variations can be made by combining effects created by spraying through and spraying around a stencil on the same card. Autumn cards can be effectively prepared by air-brushing dark blue and yellow through a stencil combined with a free treatment on cork. Christmas designs with the customary candlesticks, holly leaves, and other symbols can be rendered on silver-surfaced cardboard.

CORRUGATED CARDBOARD DISPLAYS. Interesting displays can be created with the use of corrugated cardboard made expressly for display purposes and available in various colors. The displays can be made in curved or cylindrical forms as well as flat, and given a modern air-brushed treatment that is adaptable to specially dressed show windows.

Avoid selecting corrugated cardboard with a background color that looks cheap and showy. It is best to choose a subdued color, especially for displays with large areas. Make a sketch on stencil paper of the design to be air-brushed. Cut out the stencil and fasten it in place over the corrugated cardboard, and air-brush the stencil in the shade necessary to produce the desired effect. Hold the air brush slightly away from a vertical position so the spray will not go under the stencil into the corrugated indentations.

THE AIR-BRUSHED APPLIQUE. Using the air brush to produce an illustration or design or lettering to be appliqued to a display card gives a pleasing extra treatment to what might otherwise be an ordinary piece of work. When the layout for the card is made, the portions to be appliqued are designed and air-brushed and then fastened in place on the card with glue or other means. These appliques can take the form of cut-outs of the air-brushed illustration or design. The rest of the card can then be executed with the air brush or by hand.

PROCESSED AIR-BRUSH EFFECTS. The appearance of the half-tone can be produced on screen-processed displays or display backgrounds by air-brushing the original design on the screen. There are three methods that can be used for this.

The first method: Cut a stencil for the design to be air-brushed in order to produce a sharp line on the finished work. Use a good grade of vellum paper for this stencil. Coat the stencil with diluted glue and

PROCESSED AIR-BRUSH EFFECTS. The appearance of the half-tone can be produced on screen-processed displays or display backgrounds by air-brushing the original design on the screen. Here glue is being applied with the air brush to open areas of the stencil to obtain a blended effect.

place it against the screen. Smooth out the wrinkles with a warm iron. To obtain the shading of the design, spray show-card color on the screen, placing the color where the lights and middle tones are desired. When the color dries, squeegee cutting-in lacquer over the screen. After the screen is dry, turn it over and wash it with hot water to remove the show-card color and the lacquer covering it. The screen is then ready for use.

The second method: Cut a film stencil and apply it to the screen. Place diluted tusche in the air brush and atomize it on the open part of the stencil design where the shading is desired, working in reverse. Squeegee cutting-in lacquer over the tusche and the open part of the stencil, and wash the screen with hot water to remove the tusche.

The third method: Pencil the design lightly on the screen, and shade it with air-brushed show-card color. Apply lacquer to the screen about the design, and wash out the show-card color with hot water.

WINDOW DISPLAY BACKGROUNDS. A wide range of possibilities is offered to the air-brush artist in the producing of modern display backgrounds for show windows. Seasons of the year, special events, the merchandise to be displayed or advertised, all offer suggestions for display background treatment that can be quickly and beautifully executed with the air brush.

A display background is usually a large display piece or assembly of display pieces in desirable combination and shapes placed at the background of a window display to enhance the appearance of the display and to give it added promotional value. Backgrounds appropriately embellished can often make successful, sales-producing show windows of otherwise drab looking ones, and it is in the making of such backgrounds that the air-brush artist has ample opportunity to demonstrate his ability.

BACKGROUND MATERIALS. The display backgrounds are usually made of wall board, composition materials, or of heavy cardboard with plain, fancy, or corrugated surface. Wall board and cardboard for display purposes are available in an array of colors and a wide variety of surface textures and finishes to fill any reasonable requirements. For special display purposes, materials such as velour, velveteen, satin, and burlap can be used. Care must be taken in preparing the material so that the air-brush color used will not cause stains.

PLANNING THE DISPLAY BACKGROUND. In planning the display

WINDOW DISPLAY BACKGROUNDS. A wide range of possibilities is offered to the air-brush artist in the producing of modern display backgrounds for show windows. Seasons of the year, special events, the merchandise to be displayed or advertised, all offer suggestions for display background treatment that can be quickly and beautifully executed with the air brush.

background to be made with the air brush, strive for a simplified rendering of the design. For example, the design of a large head or a large fashion figure shown with leaves exaggerated in size can be applied to a background previously coated with the air brush. A bold effect can be obtained in this manner. The most effective backgrounds are those in which few colors are used.

The first decision in planning the display background design is to ascertain the style of treatment—whether it should be a silhouette effect or a poster effect. The second consideration before the actual designing is begun is in regard to the amount of emphasis to be given to the design. A background design should be in free, flowing curves, rather than in contours that are stiff and displeasing.

DISPLAY DESIGN SUGGESTIONS. The following are given as suggestions for air-brushed designs to illustrate the possibilities for the air-brush artist in display work. These design suggestions can be applied to display cards, large display backgrounds, display pieces, floor displays, counter displays, and similar units, when the effects are appropriate to the requirements.

The making of a seasonal display for autumn, as an example, can bring into use actual leaves, which are arranged on the surface of the display in the form of a design and fastened in place with pins or thumb tacks. Shades of brown can then be air-brushed around these leaves with the color concentrated at one side and laid around the rest of each leaf in a light tone. The leaves can then be removed and the display is ready if no lettering or additional design is required on it.

SOME DESIGN SOURCES. Many everyday objects can be used to advantage in making air-brushed designs for advertising displays. Vines, lace, can tops of different sizes, the human hand, scissors, knives and forks, and anything else can be used that is sufficiently flat to insure a reasonably sharp outline when the color is applied over it with the air brush.

A study of machine parts can give the artist enough design ideas to last him indefinitely. One example is an automobile gear that is large in size combined with a small spur gear. The large gear is laid on the display surface and air-brushed in some color, such as light blue. After the color has dried and the gear is removed, the spur gear is laid partly over the air-brushed outline of the large gear and air-brushed a light yellow. An effect of transparency is gained by doing this, as well as a number of intermediate greens caused by the overlapping of the blue and yellow.

NOVEL EFFECTS. A kind of display-card background that is extremely effective can be produced by arranging a series of paint jars or cans on the display surface and spraying about them. This gives a design in curves. The air brush should be held at about a 75-degree

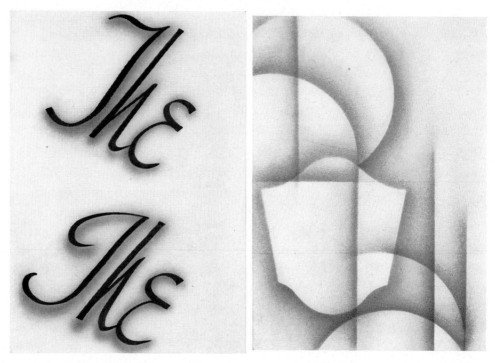

APPLYING THE AIR BRUSH. The applique effect at left illustrates how black cut-out lettering applied to a background surface is enhanced when given a pleasing extra treatment with the air brush. At right, a novel effect is obtained by air-brushing along edges of cut-out shapes laid on the working surface.

angle to the surface and at a working distance of about 15 inches.

Another novel display background design that is easily produced is made by spraying to the edge of a strip of cardboard that is placed at different angles on the display surface. In this case, the display card should be held in a vertical position.

A unique effect can be produced by laying a wire screen over the display card or background, keeping the work in a horizontal position. This is air-brushed in the desired color, with the air brush about 20 inches from the surface of the work. A concentration of the spray at the corners produces a soft vertical and horizontal pattern over the surface.

A novel display-card background can be made by laying pieces of lace on the card. These can be air-brushed with a suitable background color to produce traceries of the lace patterns on the card.

Such objects as nails, tacks, machine parts, shot, and shavings can be arranged for air-brushing to give interesting patterns. They should be first arranged in a pleasing design on the card surface, and then sprayed with the background color. When the color is dry and the objects are removed, a striking background will have been created.

MANY OTHER APPLICATIONS. There are many ways of applying air-brush art to the advertising display, in addition to those described here. The purpose here has been but to suggest some of them. Many display artists are adept users of the air brush in their work of producing attractive displays in which ingenious air-brushed effects are achieved.

In this work, experimentation is the mother of discovery. It unfolds to the artist new possibilities and reveals effects that can give artistic individuality to his work, such as is attainable with no other means than the air brush under the guidance of his own hand.

CHAPTER XIV

THE AIR-BRUSHED SIGN

THE KINDS of signs that can be readily produced with the aid of the air brush include the banner, the cloth sign, the transom sign, the valance sign, the fascia sign, the door sign, and signs that are part of the architecture of a building or store front. These signs should incorporate factors that make them easy to read, that suggest the nature of the products, firms, or services they advertise, and that harmonize with their surroundings.

THE AIR-BRUSHED BANNER. The method of preparing an air-brushed banner or a cloth sign is a simple procedure. For making small banners, outline the lettering on stencil board, cut the letters out of the stencil board with a sharp stencil knife, hold or fasten the stencil board in place on the sign cloth, and air-brush with a spray of diluted oil color. Japan color is also suitable for this purpose.

If much of this work is done, copper stencils can be made of popular letter styles in several different sizes, such as might be required. Centers of letters can be held in place by thin wire. These letter stencils can be held against the banner and air-brushed. By using a thin-gauge copper and a cutting machine, the making of these stencils is simplified.

THE AIR-BRUSHED BANNER. The method of preparing an air-brushed banner or a cloth sign is a simple procedure.

74

AIR-BRUSHED GLASS SIGN. Tube japan black was mixed with varnish and air-brushed through a stencil fastened in place on the glass.

A metal file is excellent for smoothing the cut edges.

A second method of producing the air-brushed banner is to letter it by hand and then apply air-brushed effects, such as designs, rules, letter shadows, and decorations.

Although letter shadows might be desirable on some banners, the average banner must be made in a hurry, and time can not be spent cutting stencils for the shadows. Simply hold a piece of cardboard with a true edge in place to form the letter shadows. Borders can be air-brushed around the banner with the aid of long pieces of cardboard held in place.

AIR-BRUSHED GLASS SIGNS. The new styles of architecture with ultra modern exteriors and interiors in glass and steel demand signs that are as modern as the settings in which they are placed. The air-brushed sign on plate glass is ideal for such purpose.

Air-brushed signs on colored architectural glass are very effective. There are many new colors of structural glass available and these, when combined with black and white or light-colored air-brush work, provide signs of a most unusual nature.

The glass should be thoroughly cleaned to remove all grease or dirt.

A stencil is then cut for the lettering or design and fastened in place on the glass. Tube japan black is then mixed with a good grade of clear varnish until the consistency of the color is about twice as thin as when used for hand lettering. This color is atomized through the stencil with about forty pounds of air pressure. It is necessary to clean the air brush frequently when spraying this heavy color.

After the design is thoroughly dry, a coat of clear varnish should be sprayed over it. The stencil should remain in place until the sign is completely dry. It is a good idea to dust the stencil with fuller's earth. Stencils for glass signs in quantity production should be cut in copper instead of the usual stencil board.

METAL SIGNS. Metal signs for indoor or outdoor use, like many

METAL SIGN. Metal signs can be expediently made with the air brush in the hands of the practiced air-brush artist. This sign was made by air-brushing the metal surface with two coats of flat white on which the black lettering was air-brushed through a stencil.

other mediums of display advertising, can be expediently made with the air brush in the hands of the practiced air-brush artist. After the signs are cut and the metal surface is cleaned and treated in the usual manner for sign work, the next step is to spray the color desired for the base or ground coating of the sign. Any standard, heavy-duty air brush is adaptable for this purpose.

The color should be thinned so that it can be applied evenly to the surface. When the first coat is dry, it should be sandpapered with a No. 00 sandpaper and followed with another light coat of the base color. The surface should be sandpapered lightly, and a third coat applied.

The lettering or design should then be drawn on stencil board or kraft paper and cut out. This stencil can be held in place against the sign surface by using clothespins, metal clips, or masking tape. Using an air brush suitable for heavy duty display work, spray a good grade of ground oil color in one of the following ways: By uniformly covering the area within the stencil; by shading the area from dark at the top to light at the bottom, or vice versa; by applying the color around the edge of the stencil letters, leaving centers of strokes open; by applying the color so that in each letter one side is dark and the other side is light.

Ornamental designs also can be stenciled and applied with the air brush. Beautiful letter shadow effects can also be applied.

It is possible to depart from the ordinary metal sign and produce an unusual kind of sign, modern in its appearance, by applying deep letter shadows with the air brush, or by shading the background of the sign from light to dark with the air brush and applying the lettering by hand. Another novel idea is to apply one color over another to produce intermediate effects in the letter areas, letter shadows, and other parts of the sign design.

PRODUCING A CRYSTALINE FINISH. To produce a metal sign with a crystaline finish, prepare a stencil of the lettering or design. If the background of the sign is to have the crystaline finish, then the letters that are cut out should be carefully fastened in place on the metal and sprayed with clear lacquer in which mothballs have been dissolved. This mixture should consist of about eight mothballs to a half pint of clear lacquer.

If the letters are to have the crystaline appearance, then apply the stencil containing the letter openings to the metal, and spray the mixture through the stencil. Treat the rest of the metal background by covering the letters with the original letters cut from the stencil and spraying the background with the color desired.

Effective signs can be prepared by covering wall board or composition board with gold or silver metallic paper. Cut tracery designs in a stencil and spray the mothball solution through the designs onto the metallic paper. Then letter the sign by hand with a lettering brush. Backgrounds of great beauty can be produced in this way.

INTERIOR SIGNS. The indoor directional sign must reflect the architecture of the wall or surroundings where it is placed. It must be easily read and of such a size that it can be easily seen from a distance. It can be made of wall board, composition board, wood, glass, or metal.

In air-brushing this kind of sign, cut a stencil for the design. This stencil, cut in stencil board, can be filed away after being used, so that if additional signs are needed they can be quickly made.

If the sign will be subjected to handling, spray it with waterproof ink; otherwise use show-card color. The air pressure should be thirty-five pounds for work of this kind.

The indoor sign for identification purposes is generally placed in retail stores over counters, showcases, tables, or bins where the merchandise is being shown. It is sometimes part of an elaborate diplay. These signs are of permanent nature, made of materials that will stand cleaning. Such signs can be attractively made of wall board or composition board with air-brushed background and lettering.

OTHER KINDS OF SIGNS. Valance signs can be produced by drawing the desired copy on stencil board, making a stencil, and spraying the color through it onto wood, wall board, metal, glass, or cloth.

Fascia signs, door signs, and signs incorporated in the architecture of a building can be speedily produced on hard wood or metal by air-brushing the lettering through stencils. A good grade of primer should first be applied to the surface if it is wood. This can be followed with a coat of varnish sandpapered with No. 00 sandpaper. The lettering can then be air-brushed on the sign and given two or three coats of varnish.

CHAPTER XV

AIR-BRUSHED EXHIBIT SETTINGS

THERE ARE two phases of work in the making of exhibit settings with the aid of the air brush. The first phase is the designing and drawing of the exhibit setting, and the second phase is the air-painting of the setting itself.

THE MODERN EXHIBIT. Recent years have witnessed a remarkable evolution in the design of commercial and industrial exhibits. Exhibits used to be of the "muslin-and-crepe-paper" booth variety, with little or no thought given to design, except as it related to the size of the booth to fit the space it was to occupy. For the most part, the exhibit remained an unexploited medium of advertising display.

The modern streamlined styles of architecture adopted by expositions of recent years have marked the turning point in the designing of commercial and industrial exhibits. The modern exhibit settings are built of substantial materials, and new conceptions in design and coloring are employed. It is in this new coloring of exhibit settings of today that the air brush has its important place.

ITS CHARACTERISTICS. It is perhaps well to list some of the characteristics of the modern exhibit. They are:

1. It is streamlined in its general aspect.
2. It is simplified, yet well designed.
3. The products displayed are of minimum number.
4. The products are provided with an appropriate setting.
5. Uses of indirect and direct illumination glorify the exhibit and the products.
6. It is enhanced by harmonious color combinations, some of which are possible only with the air brush.
7. It presents its messages in the modern manner, with cut-out letters, built-up letters, silhouette letters, and metal channel letters.

These characteristics must naturally be taken into consideration when the exhibit setting is being designed. Full advantage should be taken by the air-brush artist of the individualistic color treatment his use of the air brush makes possible.

MAKING THE DESIGN. It is often necessary to make two renderings of the exhibit design. The first drawing is quickly made with the air brush to show the client how a proposed exhibit will appear. This drawing need not be prepared in detail, but it should present a strikingly forceful representation of an idea that will show a particular product to best advantage.

The second and more detailed design is made after the idea sketch has been approved. This should be a correctly scaled drawing, showing measurements, lighting details, and architectural treatment.

Complete drawings of modern exhibits usually consist of three parts—an architectural drawing showing the construction, an electrical drawing showing the wiring diagrams and the voltage needed for mechanical equipment, and the sketch showing the entire exhibit design in color.

The chief things that govern the designing of the exhibit for exposition purposes are the rules and regulations of the exposition, which, for the sake of uniformity and harmony in the general scheme, establish certain requirements that must be met in relation to the kind and colors of lighting, colors of the exhibit setting, size and kind of lettering, and size and kind of illustrations, decorations or other embellishments. The designer must therefore familiarize himself in advance with these regulations so that his design will conform with the requirements.

The designer should strive for a decided center of interest in the entire design. This can be achieved by using a unique shape, such as a modernistic form or a concentration of warm color or illumination. All three of these devices can be employed at once with great effectiveness. All other elements in the design should then be made subordinate to this one principal element. It is occasionally of advantage to draw the air-brushed tones toward that one element so that the eye will be naturally led to the heart of the design.

THE AIR-BRUSHED DRAWINGS. When making drawings of an exhibit for use in modern expositions, the air brush provides the artist with a tool for rendering color and laying washes needed in the modern exhibit made with large flat surfaces and curved forms. It is the answer to the problem of how to indicate reflected illumination and indirect illumination.

AIR-BBUSHED EXHIBIT SETTING. There are two phases of work in the making of exhibit settings with the aid of the air brush. The first phase is the designing and drawing of the exhibit setting, and the second phase is the air-painting of the setting itself. This is an air-brushed drawing, the guide for the air-brushing of the actual exhibit setting.

USE OF FRISKETS. The scale of the exhibit drawing will determine the amount of masking that will be necessary. To bring out the detail in small drawings, over-all friskets will have to be laid on the drawing surface. The smallest and darkest areas should be cut out first and air-brushed, and the lightest and largest areas should be cut last.

In making large-scale exhibit drawings, no friskets are needed if a sensitive type of air brush is used. Wherever a hard line is needed, a straight-edged piece of cardboard can be held in place and the color air-brushed to its edge. Lettering that is air-brushed, however, needs to be stenciled.

MAKING THE DRAWINGS. Several problems present themselves in the making of drawings of the modern exhibit. The most important of them are considered here.

First to be considered is the representation of light and shade on a modernistic form from an indirect light source. To accomplish this, make a mask around the individual form and air-brush the surface in the color desired, making it lightest nearest the illumination and darkest away from it. Light troughs provided with reflectors just a few inches out from the surface will cause the light to be concentrated in the portion nearest to the reflector. Light troughs removed from the surface tend to produce a more uniform illumination, and consequently less air-brushed shading is necessary. If there are multiple shadows, they should be plotted from each source of illumination.

Use a pen or lettering brush to draw small lettering that is to appear on the exhibit setting. This is done after the surface has been air-brushed. If the lettering is to be extremely large, it can be air-brushed with the aid of a stencil.

Make each color the same value range. For this reason it is a bad plan to use different brands of color on the same drawing.

Phantom effects are especially useful in exhibit designs. By phantom effects is meant the rendering of the exhibit in air brush in full color and the applying of the outline of the object or objects to be displayed fainting in air-brush. These are rendered through a stencil with a flat wash effect in light gray. This is especially useful for showing proposed arrangements for the merchandise.

Indicate rather than portray human figures that might be shown grouped about the exhibit to give a realistic appearance. They should be regarded merely as atmosphere rather than part of the design.

AIR-PAINTING THE EXHIBIT. With good air-brushed drawings as a guide, the air-brushing of the actual exhibit setting should not be a difficult problem, especially if the air-painting of the setting is done by the same artist who made the air-brushed drawing of the setting. The air brush is being used with marked success in the producing of beautiful exhibit settings for expositions, automobile shows, and exhibitions of various kinds. This is principally because of the manner in which the air-brushed colors can be made to blend in the molding of the exhibit setting as a unity of modern design and beautiful coloring.

Material in previous chapters can be helpful in giving suggestions for the air-brush work, such as the chapters on form representation, lettering, and air-brushed displays, as well as the chapter in a later section on air-painting the mural.

PART IV

PORTRAITS

CHAPTER XVI

AIR-BRUSHED PORTRAITURE

THE AIR BRUSH is an acknowledged instrument of art for the creating of beautiful portraits. The air-painted portrait can be produced with such fidelity of light and shade that its smoothness and softness of tone give it a marked resemblance to a big photographic reproduction. The air brush likewise gives unusual opportunities in the laying of the planes of shade and color that compose the portrait in poster technique.

PORTRAIT ART. Air-brushed portraiture has been employed with considerable success in theatre display work. Some of the poster artists who make these air-brushed posters have become quite proficient in their art. Such renderings are very appropriate for exploiting certain kinds of motion pictures and for portraying the moods of the characters.

The air-brushed portrait has other uses, too, such as for advertisements and displays that advertise cosmetics and many other commodities, and for other advertising art work. It is also a saleable piece of art for anyone who becomes proficient in making faithfully produced enlarged likenesses from photographs of individuals.

PREPARING THE WAY. The chapters in this section of the text give thorough consideration to the making of the air-brushed portrait. This present chapter serves as an introduction to the subject, preparing the way for study of the succeeding chapters, which give detailed explanations of the air-painting of the various parts of the portrait, such as head, eyes, mouth, nose, ears, hair, and backgrounds.

AN OUTLINE OF PROCEDURE. It is well to know first the procedure in the making of an air-brushed portrait, whether it be rendered as a photographic-appearing likeness or in poster style. The procedure outlined here is for the rendering of an air-brushed portrait in grays.

Select a photograph of the subject for use in making the air-brushed reproduction. The photograph should be clear, with eyes and the mouth outlines well defined. Make a sketch from this photograph. Mark off areas of highlight and shade on the sketch, and indicate with numbers the values on the various sizes, according to the primary value scale.

Mix a wash, using ivory black water color or diluted ink and making the mixture a value 4. If the face is not in profile and if one side of the face is in shade, it is best to begin with the pupil of the darker eye, working outward, and putting in next the shade of the iris. Lighten the value for the iris area in the lower portions.

Put the upper lid line in outline and render the eyelashes out from this line. Next, carefully air-brush the shade areas beneath the lower lid and in the corners of the eye, constantly moving the air brush to prevent spotting. The eye should then be touched up to get the exact thickness and shape of the lower lid and to delineate the lines and veins in the eye, as well as small color flecks that might be present. In some portraits, these small details might not be necessary.

The next step is to air-brush the mouth, setting the adjustment to a fine spray and painting the outline of the upper lip. The exact illumination shown in the original photograph should be reproduced in this shading, although it is well in some instances to exaggerate the sizes of the highlight areas.

When air-brushing the lower lip, work upward and outward from the shadow areas beneath the lower lip. The edge of this shadow plane will form the outline of the lip. Set the air brush to an open adjustment and apply the color very lightly. Vary the working distances constantly to produce the smooth skin texture and the small shade areas that occur in the corners of the mouth and above the upper lip. Change the spray adjustment as required.

The nose can be air-brushed next. Begin with the darkest shade area and work outward and downward toward the end of the nose. After the upper shade areas of the nose are painted, begin at the nostril areas and form their shapes. Ears should be carefully sketched in the beginning. First air-brush the darkest areas in the structure and work outward. There are several methods in which the hair can be shown in air-brush, these being described in the chapter on that subject.

AIR-BRUSHED PORTRAITURE. The air brush is an acknowledged instrument of art for the creating of beautiful portraits. The air-painted portrait can be produced with such fidelity of light and shade that its smoothness and softness of tone give it a marked resemblance to a big photographic reproduction.

STEPS IN PORTRAITURE. Air-brushed portraiture has been employed with considerable success in theatre display work. Here are shown steps in the procedure of making air-brushed theatre posters after the outline sketch is drawn.

Last to be air-brushed is the background, which depends in its shape and design upon the ingenuity of the artist and upon his consideration of the circumstances in which the air-brushed portrait will be used and of the subject itself. Various kinds of backgrounds for this purpose are described in detail in the chapter on that subject.

THE TWO-COLOR PORTRAIT. The head for a two-color portrait should be selected with care. The best kind is one that has extreme lights and darks. Choosing the correct color combination is the next problem. Complementary combinations are ideal for this purpose, such as yellow-red and blue, yellow-green and purple, yellow and blue-purple. Effective color combinations can also be achieved by using black and one color, such as black and yellow, black and light blue, or black and yellow-red.

The first step in the actual rendering of a two-color head is to sketch the head and to mark off the areas of highlight and render those areas in the lighter of the two colors. The second step is to mark off the areas of the deepest shade and render them in the dark color of the combination.

In marking the values, designate them lightly in pencil from value 1 to value 9. A two-color head in yellow and blue-purple, for example, would require that values 1, 2, 3, 4, and 5 be in yellow, while values 6, 7, 8, and 9 would be in blue-purple. Extremely effective theatre posters and two-color illustrations can be produced in this manner.

The details of air-painting the eyes, nose, mouth, ears, and hair are the same as air-painting the one-color portrait as previously described. The darker tones of the color selected for the deep shade areas should be obtained by repeated air-brushing with a fairly light mixture of the dark color. Do not attempt to obtain immediately the darkest tone of the dark color.

The sizes of the highlight areas should be exaggerated in air-brushing the hair on the two-color portrait. These areas are then sprayed with the light color. Stroke a few direction lines in the high-

AIR-BRUSHING THE MOUTH. Another important step in the making of an air-brushed theatre poster is the air-brushing of the mouth. The exact illumination shown in the original photograph should be reproduced in the shading of the lips, although it is well in some instances to exaggerate the sizes of the highlight areas.

STIPPLED PORTRAITURE. These portraits were produced in an air-brushed stipple effect
with the air pressure at 10 pounds.

light areas with the darkest tone of the light color. For example, if yellow is the light color, the hair direction lines in the highlight areas would be value 5 yellow. Indicate the exact shape of the hair dress by dark directional lines in the shaded areas.

THE THREE-COLOR PORTRAIT. An ideal color combination for the three-color portrait is the split complementary harmony. This is obtained by selecting a color on the color wheel, noting its complement, and using the color on each side of this complement with the first color selected. If yellow is the color selected, the complement is blue-purple. Purple and blue are on each side of blue-purple in the color wheel. The three-color combination would therefore be yellow, blue, and purple.

A related combination is often desirable, such as sepia brown, chrome yellow, and orange vermilion. Black is sometimes used with two colors, such as blue and yellow-red, or blue-purple and yellow.

In marking all values between light and dark, values 1, 2, and 3 should be in the lightest of the three colors. Values 4, 5, and 6 should be in the middle color, and values 7, 8, and 9 should be in the darkest color. If the colors selected are yellow, blue, and purple, values 1, 2, and 3 would be in those values of yellow. Values 4, 5, and 6 would be in those values of blue, and values 7, 8, and 9 would be in those values of purple. If three color cups are used, one for each color, the work is made easier.

CHAPTER XVII

THE HUMAN HEAD

PORTRAYING the human head with the air brush presents two chief problems to the artist. One problem is that of portraying the features and planes, and of obtaining correct proportions to produce a likeness. Another problem is that of portraying facial expression.

HEAD CONSTRUCTION. Air-brush artists who expect to do considerable art work involving illustrations of human heads will be interested in studying bone and muscle construction to be outlined here. Some knowledge of the physical construction of any part of anatomy is essential to the achieving of exact and correct likenesses. It conveys a "reason why" understanding that gives the artist confidence in his ability, which in turn is reflected in his work.

EXPRESSIONS. Most of the muscles that give motion to the body extend from the surface of one bone to the surface of another. Head muscles are different; one end is attached to the bone and the other end is attached to the skin. This structure makes possible the producing of changes in facial expressions.

The artist is most often called upon to portray happiness in the faces of his air-brushed illustrations of people. This is particularly true in advertising art. In the typically happy face, the corners of the mouth turn upward and wrinkles form around the corners of the eyes. The mouth lines are deepened and the lips are full and slightly parted.

The face that shows hatred, on the other hand, has lips compressed and thin, and the mouth lines are straight. The eyes are partly closed with a decided straight line in the upper lid, and the eyebrows are lowered. Furrows between the eyes seem to pull the brows closer together, and there is a sharp indentation in wrinkles about the mouth.

The typically sad face shows drooping corners of the mouth. The eyes seem to slope downward toward their outer corners, and the face planes assume a drawn appearance. Other emotions and physical states bring about facial changes that are peculiar to them.

BONES OF THE HEAD. The contour of the head consists largely of bone structure. The basic planes of the head likewise are determined by the shape of this bony structure. The brain is protected by bones joined together in irregular lines known as sutures. On the sides of the head are the temporal bones. The forward portion of the skull is bounded by the frontal bone, which, from the artist's standpoint has three significant points in a keystone area—(1) immediately above the nasal eminence, (2) the frontal eminences located at the upper edge of the eye orbits, and (3) the plane formation from the keystone area to the temples. Joining the temple bones are the parietal and occipital bones. These form a large portion of the spherical area of the head from the external aspect.

The malar bones or cheek-bones determine the upper cheek planes, and a forward portion joining these malar bones has a thin arch bone structure known as the zygomatic arch. These bones are sometimes called the zygoma. The nasal bone is actually composed of two small bones between which is a suture. At the end of this bone is the nasal orbit. The shape of the upper portion of the nose is determined by the nasal bone.

The width of the face toward the chin is determined by the shape and position of the jaw-bone or mandible. This is divided into the superior maxillary and the inferior maxillary. The root sockets of the teeth are in this bone structure, and the positions of the teeth in the head determine in a large measure the direction of the planes of the lips.

In making a head study the artist should observe the width of the jaw-bone, the indentation in the central part of the jaw-bone from the labial view, the depth of the mandible at the point of attachment, and in the forward region the occlusion of the upper and lower teeth and the width of the arch. The positions of the eye sockets determine the distance from the eyes to the nasal eminence or to the outer edge of the frontal bone in the profile. Depending upon these positions are the set of the eyes and the angle of the planes above the upper lid.

MUSCLES OF THE HEAD. The cranial muscle covers the bone structure on top of the brain, on the forehead, and on the back of the head. Its point of attachment to the bone is at the back of the head. This point of attachment is the occiput. The other end of this muscle is free and terminates at the lower part of the forehead. The cranial muscle in the forehead region supplies action that raises the eyebrows and causes wrinkles on the forehead.

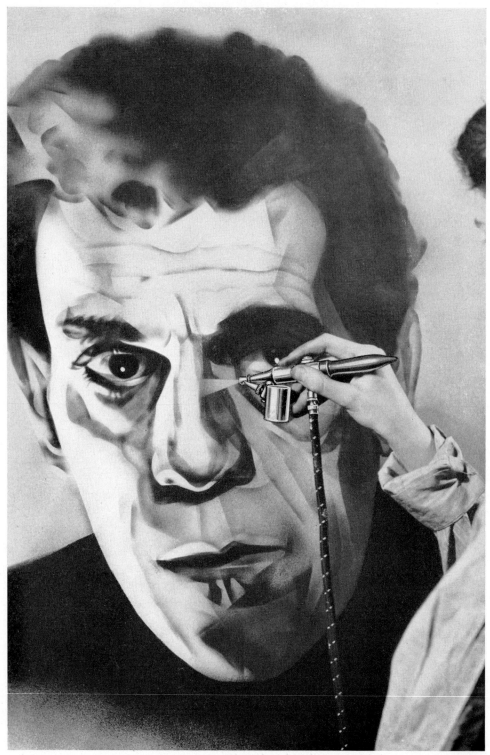

PROBLEM 1. One problem in painting the human head with the air brush is that of portraying the features and planes and of obtaining correct proportions to produce a likeness.

The position of the eyebrow on the face and the formation of ridges between the brows are determined by a muscle known as the corrugator. Facial expressions of pain, grief, deep thought, or sorrow reveal the action of this muscle. It is on the upper border of the orbit close to the nose.

Movement of the eyelids, and squinting and blinking of the eyes are caused by the action of the orbicular muscle. The orbicular muscle consists of a series of concentric fibrous rings around the eye, which join with neighboring muscles. Lifting of the upper lid is effected by a special muscle known as the levator.

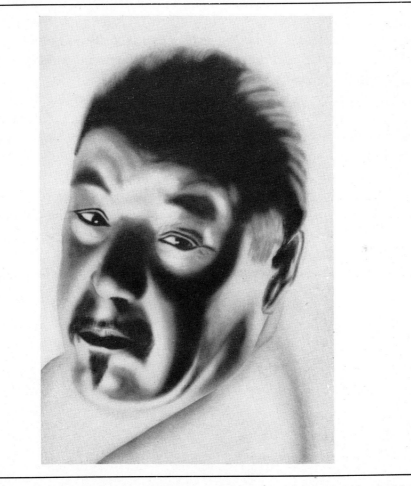

PROBLEM 2. Another problem in painting the human head is that of portraying facial expression. This illustration and the preceding one are of two distinctly different forms of theatre poster art. This example is in blended planes of light and shade, while in the preceding example the planes are sharply delineated.

The orbicular muscle of the mouth is circular in form and surrounds the mouth. Its action is to close and open the mouth. The labial fibers control the lips.

Action of the elevator of the upper lip and wings of the nose is seen in expressions of disgust in which the wings of the nose are slightly lifted. It also gives a scornful expression to the upper lip. It is limited by the upper part of the superior maxillary close to the outer surface of the orbit and by the orbicular muscle around the mouth. The angle of the mouth is determined by the canine muscle, which draws the lips upward.

The greater zygomaticus, which has its origin at the malar bone on each side of the face, runs from its point of origin across the face to the mouth corners. It is inserted into the orbicular muscle, and its action is to pull the corners of the mouth upward and backward and to change the planes of the cheek.

The elevator of the chin is a muscle that controls the position of the chin. It aids in making a pouting expression. Another muscle that functions to change facial expression is the buccinator, which is a flat, thin cheek muscle between the two jaw-bones. Part of the thickness of the cheek is determined by this muscle.

FOR LATER USE. If an artist's work in portraiture requires a more detailed study of the construction of the head, it can be obtained from books devoted exclusively to the subject of anatomy art. The information given here is intended merely to familiarize the air-brush artist with bone and muscle structures so that later work will be made easier.

CHAPTER XVIII

THE EYE

HUMAN EYES have numerous general characteristics that influence their reproduction in the air-brushed portrait. The air-brush artist should, of course, be familiar with these characteristics so that he can faithfully render them in the portrait.

EYE CHARACTERISTICS. The influencing characteristics of the eye are:

Setting of the eye;

Size of the upper and lower lid planes and their position with reference to the eyeball;

Color of the eye;

Shape of the tear glands;

Slope of the eyes with reference to the vertical center line of the head;

Spacing between the eyes;

Curve of the lower lid line;

Number of planes in the curve of the upper lid line;

Wrinkle lines in the corners of the eyes;

Flecks or spots in the iris;

Length and position of the eyelashes;

Tissue structure in the corner of the eye;

Over-hang of the eyebrow;

Ratio of width to length of the eye when it is open in normal position.

A ring muscle structure manipulates the eye, producing blinking or squinting and changing the position of the eye planes. It is in these changes that the expression of the eye is largely determined.

EYES CLASSIFIED. For our purpose, we can classify the eyes as infant, adult, and senile. The air-painting of these eyes changes from an open, rounded treatment in the infant eye to a line detail rendering in the adult and senile eye.

The texture of the skin of the infant eye is soft and smooth, and

ADULT EYE. Eyes can be classified as infant, adult, and senile. Air-painting of these eyes changes from an open, rounded treatment in the infant eye to a line detail rendering in the adult and senile eye. This is an adult eye.

the spacing between infant eyes should seem greater than between adult eyes. Chubby, indefinite upper and lower lid planes also characterize the child's eye.

The adult eye, while not showing a tremendous change in skin texture, shows clear-cut plane lines. The senile eye is characterized by puffiness of the lower lid plane, creases and wrinkles, the tendency of the lower lid to bulge or flatten, and a roughness in the skin texture.

THE EYE OUTLINE. A true portrait likeness can not be produced without an exact eye outline. Strive first to make an exact eye outline and then change it to suit the mood or expression of the individual. The vein structure in the eye should be carefully studied.

AIR-BRUSHING PROCEDURE. The procedure for making an air-brushed drawing of the eye is as follows:

Sketch the eye outline very carefully in pencil, and sketch the tear gland structure. Block in the planes of the upper and lower lids, and mark off all areas of highlight and shade on the different planes and within the iris.

Starting with the pupil and using diluted India ink, apply the color, using a slightly circular motion of the air brush and leaving a white highlight on the left lower edge of the pupil. Beginning at the top of the iris, air-brush downward, lightening the values as the lower portion is approached, and again leaving a highlight in the lower left portion. These lower left highlights in the pupil and iris are a conventional treatment and they can be varied according to the eyes of the subject.

In shading the upper lid plane, begin at the corners of the eye and work toward the center. It is best to air-paint these planes as areas rather than first to produce an outline of them. The shading on the upper and lower lid planes should show the fullness of these planes. There is a slight shaded indentation beneath the tear gland structure in the corner of the eye. The thickness of the lower lid is left light. If necessary, this light area can be made by using an ink eraser that has been cut to a knife edge.

Make creases in the corner of the eye by adjusting the air brush to a fine line. Beginning with a crease line, work outward in all directions, gradually diminishing the values until the normal flesh tone is reached. Air-brush the iris lightly enough to permit the addition of color flecks and vein structure. The tissue in the corner of the eye should be in a value 2. This gives the white of the eye a fullness for rounded form.

Eyelashes cast shadows over the upper portions of the eyes. The upper lid line is dark if there is a pronounced fullness in the upper lid

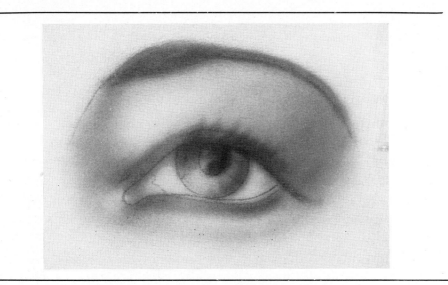

THE EYE OUTLINE. A true portrait likeness can not be produced without an exact eye outline. Strive first to make an exact eye outline and then change it to suit the mood or expression of the individual.

plane. This will likewise cause a shadow over the upper portion of the eye. This fullness will generally cause a large highlight area in the center of the upper lid plane and will necessitate the use of additional values. Overhanging eyebrows likewise shade the upper eye areas. Values in the upper plane of the eye are usually darkest nearest the nose. Creases in the eye planes should be carefully illustrated. Practice mixing colors that produce different eye colors, such as dark

AN EYE STUDY. Human eyes have numerous general characteristics that influence their reproduction in the air-brushed portrait. The air-brush artist should, of course, be familiar with these characteristics so that he can faithfully render them.

brown, blue-gray, and blue. In making the eyelash, strive for a triangular formation, the base of the triangle touching the upper plane line.

On small-scale eyes, highlights can be applied with a paint brush and reproduction white. A little pen outline will occasionally strengthen the contours. The most important thing is to have a clear outline.

THE EYEBROW. Start air-brushing the eyebrow on the side toward the nose and work outward. The area slightly below the center toward the nose is generally darkest. The tones become lighter above and below this area as the flesh color filters through the eyebrow color. This is more pronounced at the outer edges of the brow. It is best at first to place rather bold areas of light and dark. Then apply the brow lines over the areas with a sensitive air brush. If desired, this hair direction can be indicated with strokes of a sharp ink eraser.

IN THE THREE-QUARTER HEAD. In the three-quarter head. the nose plane shadow emerges into the nearest corner of the upper plane of the eye away from the observer, and the shading of the lower lid of the far eye blends into this nose shadow. The eye turned away from the observer in the three-quarter head shows a general darkening of all values. Under illumination, the eye near the observer is lighter in its general tone.

EYE TURNED DOWNWARD. When the head is tilted backward, with the chin raised, the eye is foreshortened in height, the curve of the iris is flattened, the curve of the upper lid line is increased and the curve of the lower lid line is flattened to a straight line. When the head is tilted back to an extremely high position, the curve of the lower lid may be reversed in its direction.

Air-brushing the eye in this position, all normal values on the eye are slightly lightened owing to the fact that the light rays strike into the eye. For the same reason, there is no value change between the upper and lower areas of the iris. The thickness of the upper lid shows value 1 or white and the thickness of the lower lid is not shown. The plane of the upper lid disappears in this position, and the plane area between the brow and the upper lid is lightened in value with a pronounced highlight in the center of the area. The shading on the sides of this plane is lightened in value to about half of the value shown when the eye is in the full front position.

When the head is turned downward, the upper lid line flattens to a straight line or to a curve downward, depending upon the exact position. The fullness of the lower lid is increased and the depth of the tear gland structure is more clearly shown. The values are darker on the upper lid, in the pupil and iris, and in the thickness and plane of the lower lid.

THE PROFILE EYE. Deep-set profile eyes are slightly shaded by the frontal bone structure, and this causes the values to be slightly darker in the upper plane regions. The indentation at the temporal bone causes the values to become slightly darker toward the corner of the eye. The thickness of the lower lid shows a return line structure into the eyeball. This thickness is extremely light in value. Air-brush the lashes in a triangular structure, with its base touching the upper and lower lid.

CHAPTER XIX

THE MOUTH, NOSE, AND EAR

THIS CHAPTER deals with the making of three more features in the air-brushed portrait—the mouth, nose, and ear. As with the eye, each should be faithfully reproduced from the subject if an exact likeness is to be obtained.

MOUTH POSITIONS. In air-painting the mouth, we are concerned with four general positions of the head—full front, profile, three-quarter, and tilted.

Five major line directions are usually seen in the shape of the top contour of the full front mouth. Eight lines are generally noticeable in the shape of the lower line of the upper lip in the full front view. In the lower lip, the lowest line usually presents eight distinct line directions in its contour.

In air-brushing the full front mouth on a portrait head conventionally lighted, place the highlight to the left of the vertical center line. The values gradually darken toward the corners of upper and lower lips. The creases of the corner of the mouth are from one to three values darker than the flesh tone surrounding them. The exact value depends upon the depth of these creases, which in turn depend upon the age of the subject.

If the upper lip protrudes noticeably over the lower lip, the values on the upper should be lighter than the values on the lower. In most cases, however, the values on the upper lip are darker than on the lower lip because the light is concentrated on the lower lip areas.

In the full front view of the mouth, the exact values of the planes beneath the lower lip depend upon the angle of these planes with the vertical plane. In other words, planes at sharp angles show dark values, while planes at shallow angles show light values.

If the drawing is being made in black and white, attempt to obtain an average gray value for the lips equal to the value of lip color of the subject.

The three-quarter mouth shows a definite concentration of the light

PROFILE MOUTH. This is a study of the profile mouth under conventional lighting. As with the full front mouth, the values on the upper lip are darker than on the lower lip.

on one side of the lips. One side is shortened and its value range is slightly less than for the full front position.

THE PROFILE NOSE. The profile nose presents four distinct areas when reproduced with the air brush. These are the wing area, the nasal bone area, the area from the wing to the ridge, and the area between the nasal eminence and the eye socket.

The contour of the upper half of the nose is determined by the shape of the nasal bone. The remaining contour is determined by the muscle structure. There is a well-defined wing formation that shows an indentation in the center of its area and a decided roll on the edge toward the nostrils.

The nostril should be in value 7 or 8, depending upon the amount of illumination present. The rounded portion of the nose into the nostril area should be carefully rendered with dark values near the nostril. The point area of the wing formed by the nostril structure

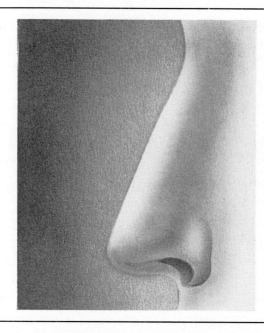

THE PROFILE NOSE. The profile nose presents four distinct areas when reproduced with the air brush. These are the wing area, the nasal bone area, the area from the wing to the ridge, and the area between the nasal eminence and the eye socket.

should be dark. The roll of the wing should present a fine line in a middle-value gray. There is a slight indentation in the center of the wing area, which should be shown by a slight darkening of the value. Since the lower edge of the wing rolls over, it is necessary to apply a line of light along this area.

In the area between the eye orbit and the nasal eminence, the values are darkened to value 4 or 5. The area between the wing and the ridge is fairly light, usually in a value 2 to 3. The range of values in the nasal bone area is dependent upon the size of the nose, the angle of the nose, the forehead plane, the width at the cheek plane across the nose, and the illumination.

A strong light whose rays strike directly upon the nose may throw that area into an absolute highlight. If care is taken with the value treatment upon the profile nose, a representation can be gained that clearly indicates the nose form.

THE FULL FRONT NOSE. The full front nose shows the width across the wings and nostrils. Extreme care should be taken in sketching the shape of the nostrils and the wing. The triangular shape at the lower termination, the side plane structure, the height of the bridge above the eye socket planes, and the change from a nearly vertical type surface at right angles to the cheek planes to an inclined surface toward the eye socket at the nasal eminence, all should be carefully shown by a subtle change in values.

In some cases, the upper planes of the full front nose are flat, while in others they are nearly vertical. The width across the bridge also varies tremendously. A highlight extends down the ridge, terminating in a ball shape at the end. The side planes in the full front view at the end of the nose show dark values nearest the cheek. The crease lines and the wings should be carefully shaded in a slightly darker value.

THE THREE-QUARTER NOSE. The true size and shape of the nostril area is shown in the three-quarter nose. In air-painting the nose in this position, first show the nostril area and the lower portions of the nose. A point is formed where the lower end of the nostril blends into the wing structure. A highlight appears on the lower edge of the wing, slightly above the nostril. An indented area toward the extreme end of the nose slightly above the nostril should be laid in with soft, intermediate tones.

There are two decided line directions in the contour of the upper line of the nostril. If a vertical line is dropped through the point of intersection of these two lines, the point of departure is determined for the plane of the upper lip. In other words, this vertical line indicates how far from the end of the nose to place the plane of the upper lip.

THE EAR. There is a great difference in the shapes of ears of individuals, and no two are exactly alike. We can, however, standardize the air-brushing procedure. The ear should be carefully sketched to conform with the subject, and in doing this the points to be observed are the angle of the ear on the head, the wall of the rim away from the skull, shape and thickness of the lobe, ratio of width to height of the ear from the profile side, internal structure, the point in the rims, and the shapes of the planes at the points of departure from the skull.

Immediately beneath the rim of the ear there is a deep-shade area and in some instances there is a partial shadow, depending upon the illumination. The lobe shows highlight in about the middle of its area, the values gradually increasing on the forward and outer sides to give the curved appearance to the surface.

In air-brushing the internal structure, apply the darkest area first,

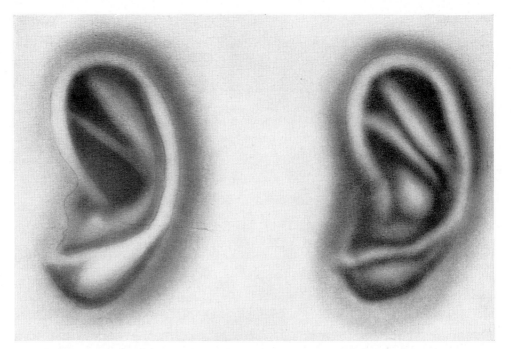

THE EAR. There is a great difference in the shapes of ears of individuals, and no two are exactly alike. There is sometimes a temptation to treat the ear in an indefinite manner rather than in the graded tones that its complex form requires.

working outward. Deep shade areas are found within the ear, due to its peculiar structure. The values in these areas are generally 7 or 8, but when the ear is on the shaded side of the head, the value is 9. The shadow structure beneath the lobe of the ear upon the neck and mandible are also dark. The shadow of the ear on the skull is generally a value 7 or 8.

The ear from the rear view shows an inclined surface which is darkest nearest the skull and light toward the rim. There is, however, a slight indentation in this area just before reaching the outer line of the rim. This indentation should be slightly shaded.

In the full front ear, the rim should be highlighted, and the value on the lobe should be slightly darker. This is true when the ear is on the illuminated side of the head. It is sometimes necessary to cut-in with reproduction white after the areas have been air-brushed.

The ear, because of its complex structure, must show as many values as any other feature or part of the face. There is sometimes a temptation to treat the ear in an indefinite manner rather than in the graded tones that its complex form requires.

CHAPTER XX

THE HAIR

THERE ARE four methods of picturing hair on the air-brushed portrait. The hair is seemingly difficult to portray with the air brush, but practice according to these methods will make the work easy. For the sake of explanation, these methods are for the air-brushing of the hair in grays, but natural colors can be used in the actual work.

METHOD No. 1. The first of these four methods is as follows:

Mark off the areas of highlight and shade on the drawing and draw in the direction lines. If the painting is of a woman, carefully outline the hair dress.

Air-brush the head boldly, using a mixture of color that will produce a value 3. Air-brush the highlight areas lightly and make the lower portions of wave areas dark. The hair should be air-brushed as if it were composed of a number of differently shaped solids in lights and shades.

Then put in the hair directions with the air brush adjusted to a line spray. The lines should necessarily be dark in the dark areas, while in the highlight areas they should be in value 2 or 3. These direction lines should appear to grow out of the forehead plane. There must be an intermediate tone between flesh color and hair showing where the flesh filters through. The lines must be closely massed together in the middle areas. They should fade into and become part of the deeply shaded areas.

The painting can be effectively touched up by using a small brush and reproduction white to sharpen highlights and the hair direction lines in the shaded areas.

On small drawings, some pen-and-ink retouching is permissible to strengthen the contours of the hair.

METHOD No. 2. The second method for rendering the hair is to block in areas of light and shade and the hair formation, lay a mask over the drawing, and air-brush through a stencil with a value 4 mixture, varying the lights and darks according to the shape of the hair.

AIR-BRUSHED HAIR. Hair is seemingly difficult to portray with the air brush, but practice according to the four methods described in this chapter will make the work easy to do.

This method is used for male heads extensively where sharp lines are desired. Blend the areas by using the air brush free-hand after the stencil is removed. If the stenciled areas are too sharp, they can be erased with an ink eraser and then air-brushed again.

METHOD No. 3. The third method for reproducing the hair with the air brush is as follows:

Using a very light mixture in the color cup, stroke in the hair direction lines, putting them as closely together as possible. Restroke these lines, using a darker mixture in the shaded portions. Cut in the highlight lines with a knife-like edge of an ink eraser. In dark areas where the hair lines are not plainly visible in the hair dress, open the adjustment on the air brush to a fairly wide spray. Using a small paint brush and reproduction white, paint in a few hair lines along the highlights to bring out the illuminated areas.

METHOD No. 4. The fourth method involves the following steps:

1. Block out the hair areas with a soft pencil to obtain the head dress.

2. Check the primary value scale against the subject and notice which values on the scale match the tones in the hair. Mark the numbers of these values on the drawing.

3. Mix as many jars of colors as you have values in the hair.

4. Beginning with the lightest color, air-brush around the highlight areas.

5. Apply, one by one, the darker tones.

6. Using the darkest value and a fine adjustment of the air brush, put the hair direction lines in the middle-value and dark-value areas.

7. With a middle-value color and a fine adjustment of the air brush, stroke in the hair directions in the illuminated parts.

8. Apply a few hair lines around the highlighted areas with a small paint brush and reproduction white.

CHAPTER XXI

PORTRAIT BACKGROUNDS

THE BACKGROUND of an air-brushed portrait should set forth the outline of the face and head, show a pattern of illumination, and contrast the head sufficiently to make it stand out from the background. There should not be so many tones in the background that they detract from the values in the head itself. Backgrounds can be classified, according to shape and method of execution, as the rectangular, oval, vignetted, highlighted, and uniform background.

THE RECTANGULAR BACKGROUND. The rectangular background is one in which the rectangle is drawn behind the head and the values are air-brushed out into the edge of the shape. This background is useful where the hard line in the background is necessary to repeat straight-line directions in a layout involving the portrait.

THE OVAL BACKGROUND. The oval-shaped background can be air-brushed with a flat wash or in graduated tones. The oval shape in itself is a beautiful one, and as a background it can be offset by breaking it about the outline of the subject. The use of an oval background sets up curved lines that repeat other curved lines in the portrait.

THE VIGNETTED BACKGROUND. A vignetted background is one in which the background color is concentrated around the subject, the values being gradually lightened into the white space surrounding the subject. This background, however, must not show so many values that it will detract from the subject.

The shade areas in the background around the subject should, if possible, repeat the outline of the subject. Complex and extreme contrast of tapering values should be avoided. In showing light and dark areas in the background, assume that a dark area exists on the light side of the subject, and that an illuminated area exists on the dark side. These areas must be placed next to the subject, and in either case the values must be blended out into the white space around the subject.

THE HIGHLIGHTED BACKGROUND. The highlighted background

is one in which white is used completely around the upper portion of the portrait. This term also applies to a background in which a strong concentration of light is present on one side or above or below the illustration. A large white area is generally employed, which tapers into values 3 and 4 on the shaded side.

A highlighted background is useful where the face tones are so soft that the addition of pronounced gray in the background would detract from them. A highlighted background is also useful where the head is in extremely dark tones.

THE UNIFORM BACKGROUND. A uniform background is one in which a flat wash is applied to the background area. For example, a portrait may be in different tones of gray. A flat wash of value 3 yellow air-brushed behind the gray head will enliven it. Flat as well as blended washes made with the air brush produce beautiful backgrounds.

A Simple Fashion Drawing. A simple fashion drawing (left) made with the air brush by sketching the figure and costume design, masking the drawing with vellum paper and frisket cement, and air-brushing. The female fashion figure (right) is eight heads in height.

PART V

FASHION ART

CHAPTER XXII

FASHION ILLUSTRATIONS

FASHION ILLUSTRATIONS are always in demand from the good fashion artist. Constantly changing fashions create a constant need for new illustrations of the fashions of the day. The air-brush artist well trained in this form of art should have ample opportunity to put his talent to good use in the creation of fashion drawings of unusual quality.

KINDS OF FASHION ILLUSTRATIONS. Air-brushed fashion illustrations can be listed under several classifications according to the use and subject of the illustrations. It is well before considering the making of fashion drawings to know these various classifications, especially those according to the manner in which the air-brushed drawing is used.

Among the kinds of fashion illustrations are, first, those seen every day in the newspapers. Closely related to those are the fashion illustrations in the magazines. Another classification embraces the illustrations used in catalogs, and still another covers illustrations in direct-mail advertising.

Air-brushed fashion illustrations made for reproduction can be divided into three groups. The first group includes those illustrations in which the air brush is employed as a simple shading medium. Simple texture renderings, such as those found in newspapers, magazines, and booklets, are also in this group.

Those illustrations that require a rather careful treatment and show considerable detail are in the second group. The third group includes illustrations that are as near perfect as it is possible for the artist to make them.

DRAWINGS FOR REPRODUCTION. Air-brushed fashion drawings for

printed reproduction are photographed through half-tone screens. The half-tone screen consists of two pieces of glass upon one of which are ruled vertical lines and on the other horizontal. These two pieces of glass are fastened together with a transparent adhesive, making a screen. This screen is placed in the photo-engraver's camera, and when the photograph is taken of the drawing, the image upon the negative is broken into small dots whose size and position register the light and dark areas of the original drawing.

The number of the screen is determined by the number of lines ruled on a linear inch of glass. Fine-line screens are used for reproducing fashion drawings to appear in catalogs and magazines printed on smooth paper. Screens for this purpose are usually 120-, 133-, or 150-line. Coarse screens, such as the 65- or 80-line, are used for newspaper half-tones and other inexpensive printed reproductions.

Fashion drawings to be reproduced by using a coarse screen should have stronger contrast of light and dark than drawings to be reproduced with a fine screen. Fine screens, such as 120-line, will pick up all the intermediate tones from light to dark that are represented on the primary value scale.

The air-brush artist should lay a light wash over the drawing with the air brush, using a light-value mixture rather than a heavy color mixture. This makes much easier the production of soft, intermediate tones.

A SIMPLE FASHION DRAWING. The procedure for making a simple fashion drawing with the air brush is as follows:

Sketch the figure and the costume design. Mask the drawing with vellum paper and frisket cement. If the costume is of one color, cut out the mask around the entire costume and remove all the excess cement from the opening with a clean cloth.

Air-brush the costume, concentrating color along outlines of the drawing and on one side of the skirt and torso. Place faint shadows in the abdominal region, in the pelvis indentions, and beneath the breasts. If the costume is close-fitting and the material has luster and clings, the left center areas of arms, legs, and torso should show white.

THE MALE FASHION DRAWING. One thing that sets off the male fashion drawing is the use of straight lines. There are straight-line outlines in the face, and long, straight lines in the creases of the trousers, as well as in the pockets and the box construction of the coat. Creases

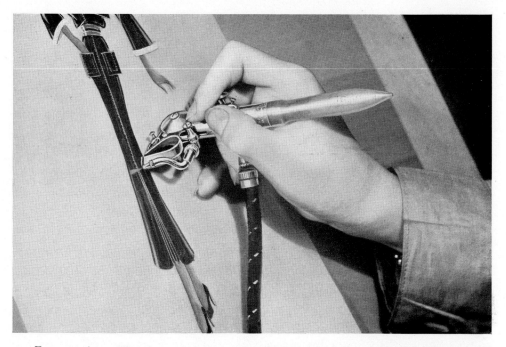

FASHION ART. The air-brush artist well trained in this form of art should have ample opportunity to put his talent to good use in the creation of fashion drawings of unusual quality. Constantly changing fashions create a constant need for new illustrations of the fashions of the day.

in the sleeves and the sleeve outlines themselves are partially in straight lines. This use of straight lines gives the drawing a mannish appearance.

The fact that the male costume is usually in somewhat standardized colors, such as grays, black, dark blues, and browns, simplifies the work. The main problem left is the representation of the texture of the material. Methods of accomplishing this are described in the next chapter.

Dark clothes as a general rule will show highlights in values 2 or 3, while light clothes should have extremely wide highlight areas in value 1. In reproducing white clothing, grays are applied only in the deep shade and shadow areas.

In showing light grays, the color mixture can be used that will produce the exact gray in one application of the color. The shadow areas and deep shade areas can be rendered in value 7 or even value 8 in some extreme cases. Shadows in lighter values should be placed under the wings of the collar, under the tie, and around the edge of the vest. Shadows help to give a soft and realistic appearance.

Pins in soft collars form indentations in the wings of the collars. These indentations should be sprayed in light gray. The head and neck will throw a shadow over one side of the shoulder, and this shadow should be in a light or dark gray.

Creases in the coat sleeves and in the cuff break line should be indicated in the simplest way possible. Simple treatment in these areas tends to give a sharp, clean-cut appearance to the suit. Such details as button holes and exposed seam lines can be completed after the drawing is finished. This work can be done with a No. 2 round paint brush.

In painting the male face with the air brush, the shadows should be a little darker than on the female face. Along the roots of the hair, there should be an intermediate gray between the face color and the hair color.

THE TWO-FIGURE COMPOSITION. Every fashion composition showing a group of figures must contain one figure that dominates the layout. It may do so by its size, position, style of costume, method of rendering, background, or by some special devices, such as lines or shapes pointing to or enclosing it.

The two-figure composition may have emphasis placed on one figure by simply making that figure erect and the other figure seated. When making an air-brushed drawing of two figures in a layout, strive for one of the following conditions:

An unusual and outstanding texture treatment in air-brush on one figure or the other;

Strong contrast between the figures and the background;

Application of gray tones in the background so that the two figures are coordinated in the design.

THE BACKGROUND. The two-figure fashion composition is most effective when some form of distinctive background is included. This background should be cut out of frisket paper or stencil board and treated in a light, indefinite manner. The dark tones should be concentrated near the figures and gradually vignetted toward the outer edges of the illustration.

Some suitable background designs are period architectural columns, a segment of a room interior, beach scenes, building exteriors, steps, a sample of textile material, silhouettes of motor cars, sport scenes, and so forth, according to the appropriateness of the design to the style of dress being illustrated.

Stippled effects are also often appropriate in the two-figure fashion drawing. These can be produced by changing the air pressure when applying the color.

THE THREE-FIGURE COMPOSITION. The three-figure fashion composition must also show one figure as being dominant. One arrangement is to have this dominant figure seated, and the other two figures standing. As the alternative, the dominant figure can be made erect, and the other two figures seated. Another treatment is to place the dominant figure in the foreground, and the other two figures in perspective in the background.

The figures should be connected with an appropriate background. This background can be related to the style of dress illustrated or suggest an occasion at which the style of dress can be worn. It can depict some scene such as those already suggested for the two-figure illustration. Modernistic and symbolic backgrounds can sometimes be used to link the three figures together.

AIR-BRUSHING PROCEDURE. The tone value on the one dominant figure should be made stronger than the values on the other figures, if possible. This can be accomplished by grouping a dark dress with two light costumes.

Strong air-brushed compositions can be made by concentrating the color at either the right side or left side, or in the middle. The right and left sides of the illustration should not present an equal gray tone, as this might cause the interest of the observer to be divided.

The outer edges of the background around the group should be made to fade gradually into the white space of the cardboard. Care must be exercised in shading behind the figures so that their shapes will not be too pronounced in a direction that does not harmonize with the direction of other parts of the composition.

The background around the feet of the figures requires delicate treatment. It is necessary sometimes to remove part of the stenciling and render the feet and these shaded areas free-hand so that they will not have a "pasted-on" appearance, but will have the natural appearance of being part of the composition.

CHAPTER XXIII

AIR-BRUSHED TEXTURES

SINCE THE ABILITY of the air-brush artist to represent textures with the air brush is a worth-while one, especially in fashion illustrations, we shall here give thought to the producing of texture effects. Texture representation has long been a difficulty for fashion artists, but with the air brush it is made easy.

CLOTH TEXTURES. There are numerous devices that can be utilized for indicating textures. When textile designs and patterns must be reproduced, some of these devices produce more exact representations than others. The secret is to know in advance and to visualize what each device will produce.

A printed textile, for example, can be reproduced by cutting out the actual design of the print and air-brushing around the cut-out, shifting the stencil over the surface of the drawing. This method gives a fairly exact representation of the pattern.

Another method is to apply rubber cement on the surface of the drawing, placing the cement where the designs occur, as if drawing the design with the cement. After the cement has partially dried, apply the air-brush color over and around it. When this color is dry, remove the cement with a soft cloth, leaving the design in white. Additional effects can be obtained by reapplying the cement and air-brushing over it again. Intermediate tones can be produced by this method.

Plaids can be produced by simply air-brushing along a straight edge, such as the edge of a piece of cardboard held in the hand and shifted in position according to the pattern to be reproduced.

ROUGH TEXTURES. To reproduce a simple woven texture, such as for men's clothing, a small stencil can be cut out of celluloid in the shape of the simple weave line, and by sliding this stencil over the surface of the suit in the drawing, the texture is reproduced. Tweed textures can be reproduced by holding small cards at different angles on the costume and air-brushing to the edges. By laying one piece of wire screen on another and twisting them, additional material weaves and

116

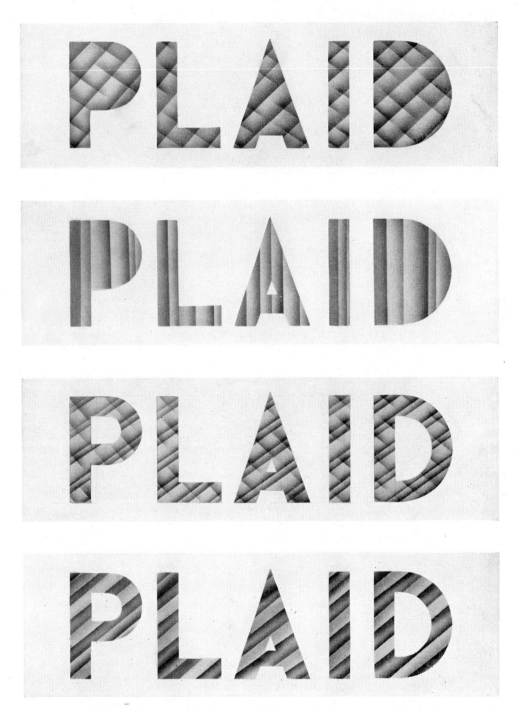

PLAIDS. Plaids can be produced by simply air-brushing along a straight edge, such as the edge of a piece of cardboard held in the hand and shifted in position according to the pattern to be reproduced.

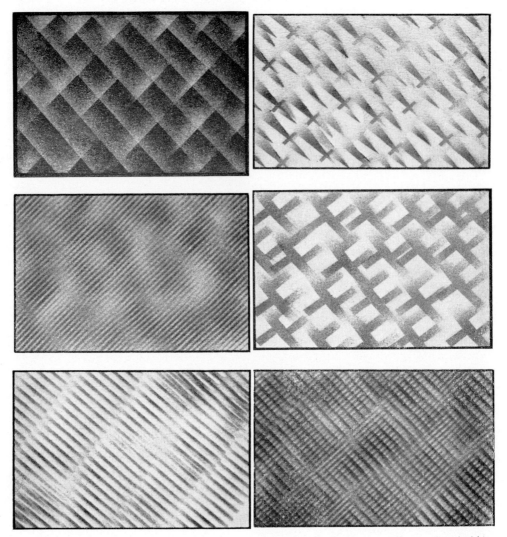

AIR-BRUSHED TEXTURES. Texture representation has long been a difficulty for fashion artists, but with the air brush it is made easy. There are numerous devices that can be utilized for indicating textures. The secret is to know in advance and to visualize what each device will produce.

patterns can be reproduced. A torn blotter edge that is sufficiently ragged is also useful.

One of the best devices for reproducing a rough tweed is an old bristle brush with part of the hairs removed. The brush is held on the drawing with the remaining hairs in place and the air-brush color is atomized over them. The position of the hairs is then changed on the surface of the drawing to give new effects.

Stippled effects can be created by placing glass beads over the surface of the drawing and air-brushing upon them. Intermediate tones can be produced by shifting the beads and air-brushing again after the first color has dried.

Tacks, nails, wire, and buttons can also be used, and a collection of screen wire and copper wire meshes in different sizes of weaves is also useful. There is really no limit to the effects than can be produced by employing these improvised materials for making shadings and patterns to indicate various cloth textures.

LEATHER TEXTURES. To produce the appearance of leather texture in the air-brushed illustration, double a piece of screen wire and lay it on the open areas of the mask where the texture is desired. Atomize the color onto the open areas. Shift the screen and apply the color again to produce an added texture effect.

Steel wool, packing excelsior, sawdust, wood chips, corn flakes, horse hair, lace, cheesecloth, and metal shot can be substituted for the screen wire to produce different kinds of textures and patterns.

TRANSPARENT MATERIALS. Transparent dress materials, such as an evening gown of sheer material under which is worn a slip, present a double problem in transparency. The shape of limbs will be apparent through the costume, and the color of the undergarment will show through the gown.

The procedure for making an air-brushed drawing of such material is to draw the figure and costume in pencil and then mask the drawing for air-brushing. Cut the mask from the body portions and air-brush in a gray equivalent in tone value to flesh color. Then cut the mask from the slip and air-brush in a gray of a tone value equal to that of the actual slip color. Remove the mask over the evening dress proper and air-brush the dress in light grays over the arms and slip just as if they were not present.

WHITE COSTUMES. To create an air-brushed illustration of a fashion figure in a white costume for half-tone reproduction, sketch the costume figure and transfer the sketch to illustration board. Then apply a frisket to the drawing and cut out the portion for the dress only. Spray a value 2 diluted ink wash with open adjustment of the air brush, keeping the tip of the air brush at a working distance of 13 inches from the surface of the drawing. Allow the coating to dry and then air-brush it again. Outline the face, arms, legs, and hands with a value 5 gray applied by hand with a No. 3 brush.

CHAPTER XXIV

FASHION ACCESSORIES

THE DRAWING of fashion accessories can be greatly enhanced by use of the air brush. Catalog illustrations of these accessories become realistic and forceful when the subtle graded tones of air-painting are applied. Accessories include shoes, hats, gloves, costume jewelry, bags, scarfs, belts, and many other items that complete the ensemble of today's attire.

HAT RENDERING. The procedure for rendering a typical accessory illustration, such as a head and hat, is as follows:

The drawing is first sketched in outline with a soft pencil on a good grade of illustration board or pen-and-ink paper. The outline is then refined and simplified to present a smart, clear-cut appearance.

If the drawing is to be reproduced on a coarse or medium-textured paper, it should be inked. The exact weight of the ink outline will depend upon the amount of reduction to which the drawing will be subjected when reproduced. If the drawing is to be reduced to one-half its original size, then the thickness of the ink outline must be twice as much as is desired in the reproduction. If the drawing is made the same size as the reproduction is to be, the thickness of the line should be equal to that desired in the reproduction.

If the drawing is to be reproduced on a coated paper, it is possible to do without the inked outline, provided that a sufficient amount of contrast is portrayed within the limits of the actual object. It is possible to give a tremendous amount of emphasis to the hat by inking it only and applying a flat tone to the face area with the air brush.

ILLUSTRATING THE SHOE. Fashion illustrations of shoes appear in newspapers, catalogs, booklets, leaflets, and on display cards. The air-brushed shoe illustration presents problems in the representation of the color of the shoe, the ornaments on the shoe, the texture of the leather, and the normal light and shade on the surfaces because of the shoe's shape.

A PLAIN SHOE. Air-brushing an illustration of a plain, patent-

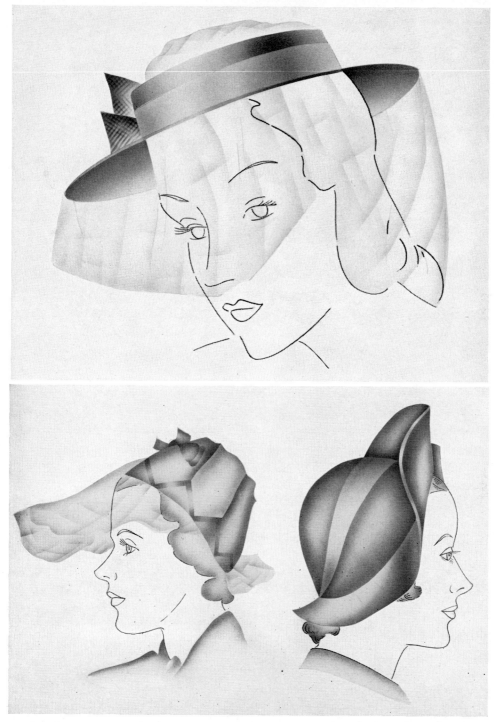

HAT RENDERINGS. The drawing of fashion accessories can be greatly enhanced by use of the air brush. In making hat illustrations, the drawing is first sketched in outline with a soft pencil on a good grade of illustration board or pen-and-ink paper.

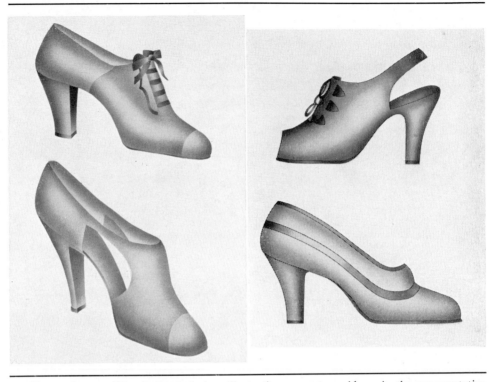

FANCY SHOES. The air-brushed shoe illustration presents problems in the representation of the color of the shoe, the ornaments on the shoe, the texture of the leather, and the normal light and shade on the surfaces because of the shoe's shape.

leather pump, for example, requires sketching of the shoe, marking off of highlights, masking the drawing, removing the mask from the vamp, air-brushing the vamp with an intense black, covering the air-brushed vamp, unmasking the sole and air-brushing it, covering the sole, unmasking all of the heel but the sharp highlight, and air-brushing the heel.

If a bow or ribbon is present, air-brush it according to its form with a slightly lighter mixture of color, and with a slight stippled effect. If the black extends too far over the highlight areas, it can be touched up with reproduction white.

A FANCY SHOE. To air-brush a shoe with embossing, cut-outs, and other detail, first make a sketch of the shoe and mark the highlights, and then apply the mask. Then unmask the vamp except where the perforations and cut-out areas are. The color value to be applied depends upon the color of the shoe.

After air-brushing the plain portion of the vamp, unmask the perforations and cut-outs, and apply a slight shading on the side away from the light. Then unmask the sole and heel and air-brush them in the same manner as already described for the plain shoe.

A TEXTURED SHOE. Next to be considered is the textured shoe—

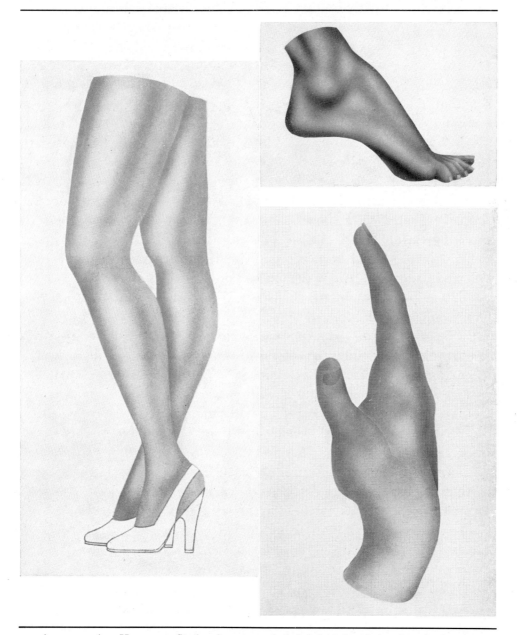

ANATOMY ART HELPFUL. Study of anatomy is helpful to the air-brush artist in portraying such fashion accessories as hosiery, shoes, and gloves.

one with leather of an unusual texture, such as alligator skin, snake hide, and rough-textured leather. In making an air-brushed illustration of this style of shoe, follow the same general procedure as already outlined for the plain and fancy shoes, except that the color should be applied very lightly in gray to obtain the form of the vamp, sole, and heel. Then obtain the desired texture by air-brushing through screen wire, copper wire, excelsior, or coarse steel wool laid over the surface. If one of these devices does not produce the desired texture, use special cut-out shapes made by drawing the leather texture on paper and cutting out the shapes with scissors. Hold these in place while air-brushing.

A TWO-TONED SHOE. Making an air-brushed illustration of the two-toned shoe requires the making of a sketch in pencil, marking off of all areas of light and shade, applying of a mask over the entire drawing, and cutting out of lightest color in vamp, air-brushing with properly diluted color, unmasking of darker areas of vamp, and air-brushing them. If the darker tone is a value 8 on the actual shoe, a value 4 color should be made and applied in successive washes until value 8 is attained. Allow the first wash to dry before making a second application. Then unmask the sole and heel areas and air-brush them as previously described.

THE HANDBAG. The making of an air-brushed illustration of a handbag is governed by the color and shape of the bag and by the kind of material of which the bag is made. We might list these materials as kid, suede, leather, alligator skin, snake skin, linen, patent-leather, cloth, beads, in addition to special materials.

First make a careful pencil sketch of the subject. This sketch must be made of the bag placed in a position that will show it to best advantage. Simplify the areas of highlight and shade and place them so that they will produce a sharp contrast. It is necessary at times to exaggerate the shapes of these areas, as well as their sizes.

Lay a mask of vellum paper coated with rubber cement over the finished sketch. Through this mask, first cut out the small details, such as straps, buckles, clasps, zippers, or snaps.

The range of grays between black and white is greater on metal than on leather or cloth and the highlight areas on metal are wider. For these reasons, air-paint all metal parts first.

In a drawing where the flap is shown as being folded over the side

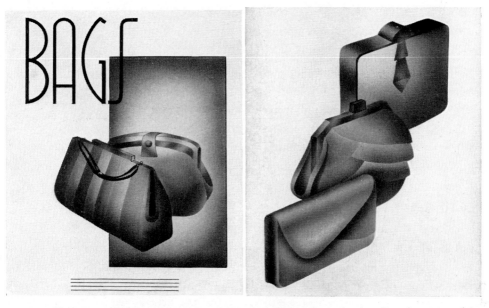

THE HANDBAG. The making of an air-brushed illustration of a handbag is governed by the color and shape of the bag and by the kind of material of which the bag is made.

of the bag, apply a slight shadow under the edge of the flap line. Creases and folds in the ends of the bag should likewise be shaded. Apply shadows to give depth and vitality to the illustration.

AIR-BRUSHED GLOVE DRAWING. The procedure for making a glove drawing with the air brush is as follows:

Carefully draw the glove, showing all details, including cuff and seam lines. Mask the drawing and cut the stencil. Apply the color of the same value as the glove to the over-all areas. Shade the fingers to show their cylindrical form. Render the shadows between fingers with a darker shade. Mask, stencil, and air-paint the details. Shade the buttons to show a quarter-moon shaded area on one side and a spot of white on the other side.

Leave wide, strong highlights on the back of the glove and along the fingers. Shade the palm of the hand rather heavily.

If the drawing is to be reduced considerably in reproduction, outline it in ink with either pen or brush. A partial outline will sometimes suffice.

Interesting effects can be produced by adding special texture designs. Lace gloves can be illustrated by simply spraying the color through actual lace onto the drawing.

CHAPTER XXV

FASHION ILLUSTRATIONS IN DISPLAYS

THERE ARE SEVERAL ways to air-paint stylish and appealing fashion illustrations for display purposes in keeping with the newest modes of window display. The air-brushed fashion drawing in display, it seems, has possibilities that have not as yet been fully taken advantage of, even by the more progressive display artists. With knowledge of illustration-making methods outlined in preceding chapters and with eyes open to the possibilities afforded by methods that produce the unique and the attention-compelling illustration, we shall now consider several ways of executing display fashion illustrations for a variety of effects.

USE OF COLOR. The chief advantage of the display fashion illustration is that the display artist is not limited by the number of colors that he can use, except as dictated by good taste. Shoe illustrations can be rendered in full color. Hats, gloves, and other accessories can be reproduced in natural colors, and dresses and other clothing can be faithfully represented.

FOR HIGH CONTRAST. In making the display illustration of the fashion figure, it is well to use high illumination. For example, the left side of the face, the upper left portion of the arms and legs, and the areas of the costume on the left side can be applied in chrome yellow. The right side of the costume can then be rendered in its actual color, and the right side of the face, arms, and legs can be air-brushed in the natural tones. This form of high contrast produces an appealing, striking illustration.

THE OUTLINE ILLUSTRATION. One method of making an unusually effective fashion illustration for display is to block out the sketch with the point of white crayon on black, blue, or pastel colored construction paper. This line should be light so that it is barely visible on the paper.

Air-paint the outline with show-card color or reproduction white using about thirty pounds of air. Use an air brush that produces a fine line spray. You can become proficient in outlining in this manner within a short time, and can improve your skill to the point where the preliminary crayon sketch will not be necessary. This, of course, would permit the making of rapidly-executed free-hand renderings.

THE PARTIALLY MASKED ILLUSTRATION. Another method of producing an illustration of more than usual interest is to sketch the subject carefully on illustration board and make an air painting by using a partial mask around only the outer edge of the costume, extremities, and head. This will produce a sharp line. Costumes and accessories that are devoid of detail can be easily handled in this way. Beautifully realistic flesh tones can be laid on the arms, legs, and face, as well as exquisite gradations of color in the actual costume. Certain styles of dresses with details will require masking, however.

THE BRONZED ILLUSTRATION. Large-scale fashion drawings modernly treated for display use can be effectively produced in the following manner:

Make a pencil drawing of the setting. Apply natural flesh tones to the exposed body parts, making the highlight areas in yellow and the shaded areas in blue or gray. Air-brush the costume with a binder for bronze, silver, aluminum, or gold powder. Apply the powder with the air-brush powder gun while the binder is still tacky. After the drawing is dry, dust off the excess powder and paint in the facial features with a small paint brush. As a novelty, the metallic powder can be applied to the body parts, and the costume air-brushed in its natural color with a fine grade of opaque paint.

THE DUOTONE ILLUSTRATION. Good results in air-brushing the display fashion figure can also be obtained by using just two colors. The face, arms, and legs, for example, can be in different tones of blue and the costume itself can be in different shades of brown.

THE PARTIALLY OUTLINED ILLUSTRATION. Simple display illustrations can be rendered with the air brush by outlining all parts of the drawing except the item being merchandised. This part can be rendered in full color, using all the shades required to give form and texture.

THE TINTED ILLUSTRATION. Another simply executed fashion illustration for display use can be made by air-brushing tints to the different areas of a pen-and-ink drawing. This style of execution lends itself naturally to simple color schemes.

PARTIAL BACKGROUNDS. Partial black or deeply colored backgrounds air-brushed behind the illustration can often be used to advantage in making the subject seem to stand forth from its background, thus giving emphasis to the subject.

DISPLAY BACKGROUNDS. Display backgrounds are making a niche of their own in modern store window and interior display presentations, and of these, the air-painted background—easily and quickly made—has its own place of distinction. Sales, styles, the seasons, Christmas, Easter, special events, all are subjects for displays in which the large, air-brushed background piece can have a helpful part in the achieving of the purpose of the displays—to arouse favorable interest in the merchandise displayed and to be instrumental in conveying that interest into the store.

BACKGROUNDS. The background of the modern window display is not necessarily limited to plane surfaces nor to utilitarian materials, such as ordinary wall board. The surfaces can be curved, angular or streamlined, but not to such extremes that the background would attract attention away from the merchandise in the display instead of causing the merchandise to be enhanced.

Metal, glass, metallic papers, wood, and synthetic materials properly employed can be utilized to give individuality and quality to an otherwise ordinary display setting. Materials that should be given first consideration are the specially surfaced papers, fancy cardboards, corrugated papers, specially coated wall boards, and bent wall boards, all made especially for display purposes.

SEASONAL BACKGROUND THEMES. Air-brushed seasonal display backgrounds are very effective in giving desirable atmosphere to display presentations of the new modes in men's, women's, and children's wear. An effective yet simple and rapidly made background illustration of seasonal nature can take, for novelty, an indefinite form sufficiently suggestive to give to the display proper the desired atmosphere. Such suggestive renderings could be monochromatic or in more than one color, as desired. For autumn, as an example, sepia tones air-brushed on a cream background produce a desirable combination.

Suppose the month is November and the display is to be devoted to sports wear. Here the illustration on the background piece can be an air-brushed rendering to indicate two or more football players and a portion of the playing field. Over this, a greatly enlarged football can be air-brushed lightly with a transparent leather-tan color through

MASKED ILLUSTRATIONS. Fashion illustrations of costumes and accessories devoid of detail can be easily air-brushed in silhouette by using a partial mask. Attractive air-painted display backgrounds can be quickly made in this way.

which the previously made illustration would be visible. If the players and field are air-brushed in a color such as magenta, blue, or light green, the illustration will give an enlivening, contrasty effect that should be desirable for the kind of merchandise being displayed.

UNIQUE PATTERNS. The air-brush artist has more opportunity to take advantage of unique renderings than artists working with any other method of artistic color application. The window display background is one form of display that permits him to apply his ingenuity as well as his air brush for the achieving of something really different. He can run the gamut of renderings from the extremely simple drawing or decorative treatment for accessories, to the extremely novel rendering that signifies smartness and sophistication in the styles displayed.

Geometric shapes can be employed to create myriad designs for the ultra-modern display background. Circles, triangles, and ellipses can be utilized to produce many original patterns. Cut-outs of the shapes should first be made, and these can be air-brushed in one or more colors or in different shades of the same color.

Repeated air-brushed drawings of the merchandise displayed can also be used effectively on the background. If a display is devoted to handbags, for example, cut-outs can be made of the various shapes of bags on display, and these cut-outs can be air-brushed on the background in multiple design.

Multiple background designs are sometimes highly suitable for giving seasonal atmosphere to a display. Actual leaves and flowers can be laid on the background and color applied about them with the air brush to produce original multiple patterns of distinctive seasonal nature.

BACKGROUND LETTERING. Air-brushed lettering in large scale and in a contrasting color, consisting of initials or one or two words can also be used effectively on the display background piece. Use of such lettering is a good method of giving emphasis to the subject of the display.

PART VI

ILLUSTRATIONS

CHAPTER XXVI

AIR-BRUSHED ILLUSTRATIONS

AIR-BRUSHED illustrations can be applied to any form of illustrative art. The very extensive use to which the air brush can be put in this work makes impracticable the discussion of every possible application, but we can deal here with what we might term a cross-section of general illustration work.

CARTOONS AND CARICATURES. Cartoons can be classified as political, historical, social, economic, and miscellaneous comic. Many cartoons are not comic, but are in reality a simplified form of serious illustration in which a story or an idea is presented. In some cases, the illustration is highly decorative.

There is also the caricature, in which exaggeration is given to some peculiarity in the facial or physical appearance of a person. We can also occasionally classify cartoons and caricatures according to the kind of pen-and-ink line used for them. For example, there is the increased line, the continuous line, the accented line. The same kinds of line treatment can be applied with the air brush.

AIR-BRUSHED TREATMENTS. The cartoon or caricature sketch can first be made in pencil, and then inked with the artist's type of air brush adjusted to a line spray and held close to the drawing. The color mixture should be half ink and half water for this outline if a continuous line is used. For the accented or increased line treatment, a more dilute solution should be used, such as one part ink and two parts water. This is applied first as a line, and then by air-brushing again over the outline to produce the increased or accented line treatment.

Drawings made in this style are particularly effective and are extremely simple to make. The air-brushed outline, of course, is softer and more pleasing than the usual pen or brush line. By working in from the edge of the outline, a three-dimensional effect can be produced that adds materially to the effect of the drawing.

A striking and unusual style of drawing can be produced by outlining the figures of the composition with the air brush and then spraying the background in flat tones. The contrast of a line with the poster type of treatment emphasizes each part of the composition.

CARICATURE HEADS. In making an air-brushed drawing of a head in caricature style, choose one of three treatments—an outline drawing, an outline partially air-brushed, or areas air-brushed between the outlines.

The outline drawing tends to preserve the vitality and freshness of the idea. A slight amount of shading in from the outline gives the drawing a more realistic appearance. The outline does not have to be entirely air-brushed. It can be made in a pen or brush outline combined with air-brushing.

If the subject's ears are large and the purpose of the caricature is to exaggerate them, air-brush the entire head except the ears, and draw the ears with pen or brush outline. This will exaggerate them all the more by virtue of simple contrast. The same is true of any other feature exaggeration.

A treatment that can be used where a background is involved is to make the figure entirely in air-brush and the background in pen or brush outline. The reverse of this can be used also, with the figure in pen or brush outline and the background in solid air-brushed areas softly indicated.

DISPLAY CARICATURES. Shapes cut out of stencil board are extremely useful in making large-scale illustrations in caricatured style to be used for display purposes. In making a large outlined head, air-brush around the edge of a cut-out to make the eye, or air-brush to the outline of a cut-out circular opening to form the eye drawing. Unusual effects can be produced by combining masking with free-hand air-brush work.

ANIMAL ILLUSTRATIONS. Air-brushed art lends itself beautifully to the creation of animal illustrations. To produce a drawing of a dog, for example, make a pencil sketch of the animal, blocking out its outlines in squares, rectangles, and triangles to obtain the proportions. Study the animal from the standpoints of over-all proportions, shapes

CARICATURE HEADS. Air-brushed caricatures are easy to make. A three-dimensional appearance is given to the heads when the air brush is used to portray features and to accent characteristics.

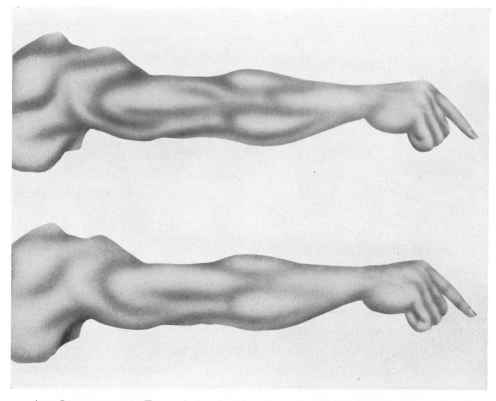

ARM ILLUSTRATIONS. Every air-brush artist who makes illustrations is often assigned the work of depicting strength in the human right arm. These examples indicate how the theories of shading the basic geometric forms are applied—the cylinder, cone, sphere, prism, and indented surfaces.

of muscles in repose, kind and length of hair on different parts of the body, positions of the muscles when the animal is in action, and the play of light and shade upon the contours of the body.

AIR-BRUSHING PROCEDURE. Draw the actual outline of the animal, and lay a piece of vellum paper over the drawing. Cut out the darkest spots first and air-brush them. Cut out the eyes and air-brush the upper parts dark and the lower parts light. Cut the shadow areas in ears and air-brush from the middles of these areas outward, gradually making the tones lighter. Cut the nose area and first lay a smooth wash over it, and then apply a stipple to obtain the exact texture.

Cut the stencil for the paws and toes and air-brush them, reproducing the hair of these parts by using a fine adjustment of the air brush to make a fine line spray. It will be necessary occasionally to sharpen these lines by applying the color to the edge of a card. The lines should be made, however, so they will not look too stiff.

One of the most vital points is to show the muscles of the legs and the areas where they join the body. The leg muscles must be carefully rendered or they will appear stiff.

Hair effects can be produced by air-brushing the edge of a stencil that has been cut in the direction of the hair.

MULTILITH WORK. Multilith reproduction is being used more and more in the production of advertising literature. In this medium, air-brush art is being employed to good advantage. The drawings for this work may be prepared as ordinary air-brushed drawings, except that a strong contrast of values should be shown. The original drawing is photographed and the negative is transferred to the zinc plate. The inexpensive way to produce the drawing is to make the air-brushed painting directly upon the zinc plate. This latter method is the one generally used today.

One procedure in applying the drawing directly to the plate is to sketch the subject lightly on the plate with a pencil containing red lead. The red lines will not reproduce. The design is then air-brushed to the red lines. Another procedure is to cut the stencil for the design and hold it against the zinc plate for air brushing, being careful not to touch the plate with the fingers.

GREETING-CARD ILLUSTRATIONS. The importance of the greeting card has increased through the years as a means of expressing greetings and good wishes on various occasions. The manufacture of greeting cards has become a thriving industry. Makers of greeting cards are constantly searching for new designs and art mediums. The employment of air-brush art has steadily grown in greeting-card illustrating.

The air-brushed illustration for greeting cards can be made entirely with the air brush or it can be partially made with the air brush in combination with some other art medium. An artist's air brush of almost any type can be used for making such illustrations. An inexpensive air brush is sensitive enough for most requirements in such work.

THE AIR-BRUSHED DESIGN. The procedure for making an illustration for a greeting card in which the entire design is to be air-brushed is as follows:

Make a thumbnail sketch of the design, make a master sketch, and render the master sketch in color, simplifying the number of colors in the design. Note the color separations necessary, black the reverse

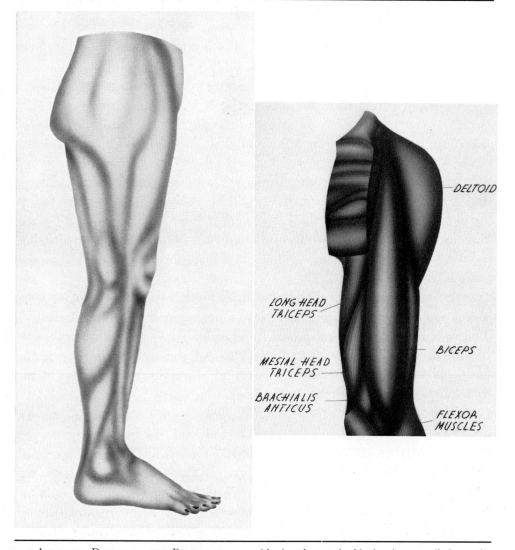

ANATOMY DRAWINGS FOR REPRODUCTION. Air brush art is ideal when applied to the making of drawings of anatomy for reproduction purposes in books, on charts, or in advertising.

side of the drawing and trace each of the colors on a sheet of oil stencil board, and cut the stencils. Mix the colors desired, using water colors, inks, or prepared air-brush colors, and apply each color through its stencil, working from the warm colors to the cool colors.

In planning the color separation of stencils, use should be made of color blending so that when red is sprayed over yellow, for example, a yellow-red will result.

CHAPTER XXVII

SURFACE REPRESENTATION

SURFACE REPRESENTATION is one of the most difficult tasks that confronts the artist. Most artists who fail in surface representation do so because of a lack of knowledge in the method of approach. The portrayal of textures, wood, marble, satin, plaster, glass, concrete, ice, velvet, steel, copper, and chromium presents real problems in illustrating. Methods of showing surfaces in air-brushed art work are described in other parts of this book, and the subject is further emphasized here because of its importance.

Two Basic Laws. Before the artist can begin any serious consideration of surfaces, he should know two basic laws:

The value of the color of the surface must be judged in the light of its gray equivalent. For example, the gray equivalent of yellow is value 3. A smooth value 3 surface will readily reflect light. Yellow likewise will reflect light to a great extent. Purple, on the other hand, has a gray equivalent of value 8. Consequently, the absorption powers of purple are far greater than the reflection powers.

The second basic law of surface representation is that the exact texture of a surface tends to be less apparent in the extreme highlight areas and the extreme shade areas. The peculiarities of texture die as they fade into the deep shade regions. For this reason, the texture of a surface is shown most plainly in the middle values areas. There must be no sharp line of demarcation, however, between the texture of the middle value areas and the textures of the highlight and shade areas. One must blend into the other.

Studying the Surface. In rendering any surface, whether in black and white or in color, these questions should be considered and answered in the artist's mind:

How does the surface affect the illumination upon it from a standpoint of the amount of light reflected and the direction of the reflected light? Is the light broken by the texture of the surface? Does the texture absorb or partially absorb the light? Is the light reflected

137

back and forth between the particles or projections that constitute the surface? Does the light penetrate through the surface? Is the light refracted as it passes through the surface? What, if any, is the shape and the direction of the surface material? What is the base color of the material and what variations in color will be necessary to represent the surface and the illumination on it? This is in reality the point at which the air-painting technique becomes truly essential.

PORTRAYING SURFACES. In pen-and-ink art, the direction and character of the pen lines portray the smoothness or roughness of the surface material. The use of the short, broken line provides a device for showing a rough surface. Patch lines, cross-patch lines, and vertical patch lines are the keys to rough-textured treatment. In air-brush painting, the same short lines varied in their directions can be used for rough-surfaced representation.

One of the most useful methods of producing a rough surface is to atomize the color through fine meshes of copper screen wire. By superimposing one piece of mesh on another and twisting the second piece ever so little with reference to the first and atomizing through them, a texture suitable for rough material, such as tweed, can be achieved.

The weights of lines, streaks, or flecks must be sufficient to withstand the process of reproduction. For this reason, it is well to keep all drawings with decided textures from one and one-half to two times the size desired when the drawings are made for reproduction. Where the detail is not too small, the drawing can be made actual size. Likewise, an extremely delicate treatment should not be used for a drawing to be reproduced in illustrations printed on coarse paper or the detail will be lost in the process.

CHAPTER XXVIII

PRODUCT ILLUSTRATIONS

ALMOST EVERY advertiser relies largely in advertising campaigns upon the picturing of products as strong selling aids. The illustrations make a direct appeal to the buyer to purchase the products by presenting their visual aspects. Illustrations of this kind are carefully executed, requiring great pains on the part of the artist to produce the exact proportions of the object and the exact texture and color value of the material itself. The air brush is naturally an excellent instrument for the artist to use in obtaining realistic treatments that are otherwise impossible.

METHODS OF PRODUCT APPEAL. Many objects are sold by means of advertising matter that contains an illustration of the object and a sufficient amount of descriptive copy or sales argument to impress the reader with the merits of the object. To present actual illustrations of such objects is to make use of the direct-appeal illustration.

Another method of product representation is by means of the indirect appeal, which plays upon some quality of the product, suggests the product, is associated with the product, or shows a state of being that the product is capable of producing. A drawing of flowers may be used to advertise perfume, or a drawing of a polar bear on ice may be used to advertise electric refrigeration.

The indirect-appeal illustration is often created to appeal to one of man's basic senses, such as taste. Sometimes it is based on social or group ideas, such as patriotism, love of the land, home ownership, and love for an offspring. Human beings are usually attracted by the portrayal of youth. This form of appeal in illustrations shows babies, children, pretty girls, puppies, kittens, and other representations of youth.

FOOD ILLUSTRATIONS. The advertising of foods has increased greatly in recent years. Illustrated advertisements of pickles, olives, soups, canned goods, fruit juices, beverages, and the like have provided much business for the creative artist.

139

The main points for the artist to incorporate in food illustrations are attractive eye appeal and a strong appetite appeal. Most food illustrations that are to be reproduced in a magazine advertisement call for full-color rendering in order to give the foods a realistic appearance. Occasionally, however, where the product is illustrated by itself, fairly effective results can be obtained with a one-color plate. Some products, however, must be rendered in different values to give them the correct form. The air brush is an ideal medium for this work.

TWO-COLOR ILLUSTRATIONS. Many product illustrations can be made to require only two colors for reproduction. The choice of the two colors will determine whether or not a good reproduction can be made from the illustration. In certain combinations of colors, when one color is blended with another the resulting color will not reproduce in its true value.

If the complementary colors, blue and orange, are used, the blue over the orange produces areas of blue-gray whose values are such that true reproduction is almost impossible. Orange might be used for highlight color on a head to advertise hats. The shade area is air-brushed over the orange with blue. In the original illustration, the area between the orange and blue is naturally a middle value area between highlight and shade which represents the normal flesh color of the head. This area appears to be a soft middle tone. In the reproduction, however, this area will appear to be a highlight area instead of a middle value area.

The second cause for this distortion of the original color is in the failure of the half-tone screen used for the reproduction to register the intermediate tones. Coarse screens do not register these intermediates so well as fine screens. The best procedure in making the two-color illustration is to select a pair of colors to produce an intermediate that photographs in its normal value.

Yellow-green and purple combined will produce deep green-brown whose value is such that it can be reproduced. Ideal two-color combinations for photo-engraving are black and yellow, black and red, and black and blue, using black for the deep and middle value areas and blue for the highlight and intermediate areas.

THREE-COLOR WORK. Three-color reproduction consists of two colors and black, or three colors such as red, yellow, and blue. The easiest rendering with the air brush is in the use of black and two colors.

PICTURING PRODUCTS. Almost every advertiser relies largely in advertising campaigns upon the picturing of products as strong selling aids. The illustrations make a direct appeal to the buyer to purchase the products by presenting their visual aspects.

This combination generally produces a strong reproduction as the dark tones in the black are sharp enough to strengthen the illustration. Certain subject matter can be easily adapted to three colors. The subjects that can be best illustrated with red, yellow, and blue are those in which a great amount of contrast is not needed and yet in which a very realistic appearance is desired.

FULL-COLOR ILLUSTRATIONS. Many product illustrations used in modern advertising are in full color. In most cases, these are reproduced by the four-color process of photo-engraving. The air-brush artist should select color tones and color intermediates that can be reproduced when illustrations are photographed through the color filters to produce the four-color plates.

The great danger in air-brush work for full-color reproduction is in the use of color intermediates that will not reproduce. The easiest

AN AIR-BRUSHED LAMP ILLUSTRATION. The air brush is an excellent instrument for the artist to use in obtaining realistic treatments that are otherwise impossible.

Light blue, when air-brushed over other colors, often produces intermediates that will neutralize, making difficult their true reproduction. way to avoid difficulties is to avoid blue overlays on the illustration.

MECHANICAL ILLUSTRATIONS. Mechanical illustrations embrace

the portraying of machines, auto accessories, parts of airplanes, motor-cycle parts, tractors, harvesting machinery, oil drilling rigs, electric motors, elevators, pumps, and other machines and objects of a mechanical nature. The chief problem of the artist is to make line drawings that show all the parts and the details of construction.

PORTRAYING METALS. Another problem is to represent such materials as bronze, copper, steel, aluminum, cast iron and other metals. Cast iron, for instance, does not reflect as much light as steel. In

MECHANICAL ILLUSTRATION. In this work, the chief problem of the artist is to make drawings that show all the parts and the details of construction. Another problem is to portray different metals.

painting a cast-iron machine with steel parts, the steel is brighter and shows more shades of gray. This representation of steel calls for sharp highlights and narrow lines of shade.

The value range used to represent bronze is white for highlights, value 3 gray for the base or average value, and value 6 for the line of maximum shade. This is the value range for a bronze cylinder, and is the typical treatment used for this metal. Cast aluminum and copper have about the same value range as bronze. Turned steel should be represented with a white line of light and a black line of maximum shade.

Because of the intricate detail in some mechanical illustrations, they can be made best with pen and ink, the air-brushed color being on the background. This color needs to be vignetted from light to dark, the light portion being near the subject and the dark portion being around the outer limits of the background. The air brush is also effective for laying washes on pen-and-ink illustrations to separate parts of the drawing. Small areas can be left in pen-and-ink shade lines while other parts can be air-brushed.

PHANTOM TREATMENTS. In some mechanical illustrations, the phantom treatment is especially useful. A differential of an automobile can be rendered with pen and ink, while the housing about it can be shown in a light air-brushed wash. This makes the gear stand out and yet shows its relation to the rest of the transmission. In like manner, a carburetor can be drawn with pen and ink and shaded with the air brush. The manifold and the rest of the engine can be indicated in a light air-brushed wash. This would show the relation between the carburetor and the rest of the motor.

CHAPTER XXIX

FURNITURE ILLUSTRATIONS

FURNITURE ILLUSTRATIONS may be classified according to use as illustrations for newspapers, catalogs, folders, or booklets. The rendering of furniture illustrations with the air brush resolves itself into the choice of a perspective angle that will glorify or dramatize the furniture, the correct delineation of the object in perspective, and the suggestive representation of surface, molds, carving, wood surfaces and finishes.

THE PERSPECTIVE ANGLE. The perspective angle is that angle in which we are accustomed to viewing an object. This provides for the "law of expectancy." This law of expectancy in illustrating refers to our past experience in which we have formed a mental image of the position in space and a general shape concept of most objects that have been about us. We expect to see a chair in a perspective angle that will show that it is resting on the floor. We are unconsciously disturbed by a perspective placement of a grand piano that elevates it above our heads. We anticipate before seeing, to a certain extent, the space relations and space positions of most objects with which we are familiar. The artist who violates these space relations in his pictures risks incurring the disfavor of the observers. We can occasionally, however, violate this rule of perspective placement for the sake of producing emphasis or attracting attention, but this style of treatment must be carefully handled.

AIR-BRUSHING PROCEDURE. When a piece of furniture has been sketched, the next procedure is to lay a frisket over the drawing and air-brush the base color. In a black-and-white representation, a value 3 gray should be the tone used to represent light oak with the grain of the wood applied in a darker value, such as 6. There should be some accents of value in this grain line. In representing dark mahogany, the base value should be of 6, with the grain of the wood in value 7 or 8.

If an extremely sensitive air brush is used, small ornaments and carvings can be air-brushed without the need of a frisket. In small

FURNITURE ILLUSTRATING. The rendering of furniture illustrations with the air brush resolves itself into the choice of a perspective angle that will glorify or dramatize the furniture, the correct delineation of the object in perspective, and the suggestive representation of surface, molds, carving, wood surfaces and finishes.

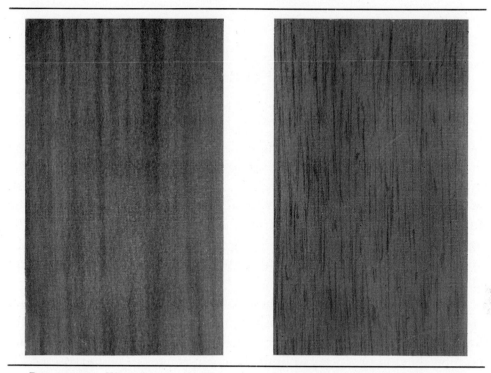

REPRESENTING WOOD SURFACES. The representing of wood surfaces requires first the ascertaining of the over-all base color to use. Woods of various kinds show grains in different colors, lighter in some woods, and darker in others. Some of the harder woods, such as mahogany and walnut, show small color flecks that should be reproduced.

drawings, it is necessary to stencil the details to produce clear outlines. When a piece of furniture is lacquered or enameled, the grain structure is covered, and the surface is reproduced from a standpoint of light and shade, merely by shading, according to the laws of basic form representation. The shading depends, of course, upon the power of the surface to reflect light.

REPRESENTING WOOD SURFACES. The representing of wood surfaces requires first the ascertaining of the over-all base color to use. After the base color has been mixed, apply it with the air brush over the entire surface, varying the values of this color according to the laws of shading the basic forms. When it is dry, mix the different values of grain color and apply these over the base surface, one by one.

Apply white flecks by using reproduction white and a pen or by using reproduction white in a sensitive air brush set to a line adjustment. If preferred, they can be produced by erasing with a ruby red eraser cut to a fine point.

CHAPTER XXX

MONUMENT ILLUSTRATIONS

SO WIDE a range of air-brush application is required in the making of air-brushed monument illustrations that knowledge of the details of this form of illustration work is valuable to the air-brush artist. Monument illustrations consist of the sales sketch and the illustration for printed reproduction. Because of its capability of producing subtle tones and blends, giving the rendering of marble and granite a realistic appearance, air-brushed art is most appropriate for making monument illustrations.

THE SALES SKETCH. Of the two kinds of monument illustrations from the standpoint of air-painting procedure, there is possible in the first, the sales sketch, a greater variety of color effects, as there are no reproduction processes to limit the color range. The purpose of the artist should be to make a clean-cut presentation of the design, tempering it with a background of color to give a cheerful atmosphere as well as one of beauty and fitting dignity.

AIR-BRUSHING PROCEDURE. Since the average monument is built of granite or marble that presents a variety of gray tones, the illustration of the stone itself is largely an air-brushed drawing in grays. Mask the entire stone with a frisket, cut out the shaded side and spray with black diluted sufficiently to give the proper gray tone. By working with a rather thick mixture of color and by holding the air-brush nozzle about 12 inches from the drawing, a rather rough granite surface representation can be achieved. A smoother surface representation can be obtained by using a thin color mixture and a fairly fine adjustment on the air brush tip.

Working on the illuminated side of the stone, concentrate the color on those portions of the area at the greatest distance from the observer. In some instances, it is advisable to use the plan of illuminating the middle of the area. For reflected light effects, sunlight effects, and stone color effects, follow the initial gray treatment with a light application of chrome yellow, Italian pink, or a mixture of canary yellow

MONUMENT ILLUSTRATIONS. So wide a range of air-brush application is required in the making of air-brushed monument illustrations that knowledge of the details of this form of illustration work is valuable to the air-brush artist.

and a light vermilion. The choice of color depends upon the effect desired. Keep in mind the illumination plan of the drawing, the possibility of reflected lights from the background, foreground, or middle ground, and the average over-all value of the drawing.

The procedure for air-brushing the shaded side of the stone in the sales sketch is to remove the mask from those areas, and to work in the consistency of black that will produce dark values. Concentrate them along the outlines nearest the observer with the subsequent lightening of values in the removed areas.

For illustrating sand-blasted panels and surface carving, remove the mask from those portions with extreme care, and change the color mixture and amount of spray to produce a different texture in stone color. The values of these areas are naturally darker than the smooth surface of the stone, unless the stone is dark. In the treatment of shape carving, treat the carved depressions in light and shade with care to

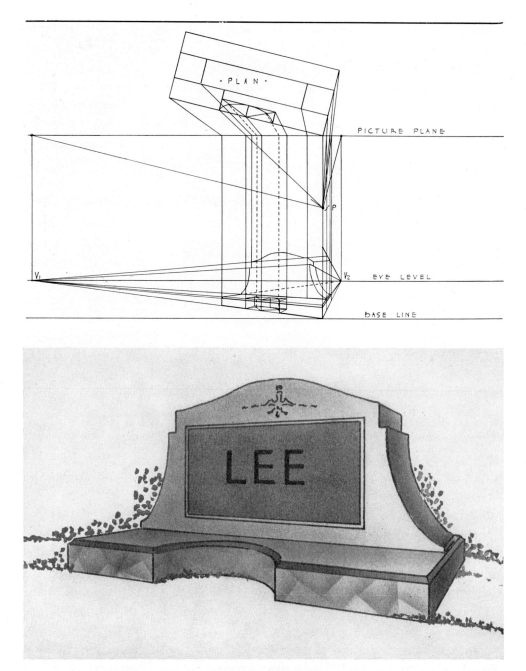

THE SALES SKETCH. The purpose of the artist should be to make a clean-cut presentation of the design, tempering it with a background of color to give a cheerful atmosphere as well as one of beauty and fitting dignity. The line drawing (above) illustrates the method of obtaining proper perspective.

reduce to a minimum the amount of hand retouching. For this purpose, use an extremely sensitive air brush with the tip set to a fine adjustment and held close to the working surface.

Traceries or patterns formed in the stone can be shown in several ways—by spraying lightly along the edge of a piece of cardboard cut into a regular curve to represent the pattern, by laying thin scraps of lead over the surface and spraying them lightly to show a pattern, or by using a fine adjustment on the air brush and simply applying the traceries free-hand. This last method produces the softest markings.

THE BACKGROUND. The secondary part of the air-brushed sales drawing is the background. The usual type of monument background consists of trees, foliage, and flowers. The lawn about the stone should be sunlit. The upper portion of the background foliage should likewise be treated with strong illumination. After the background has been drawn on the sketch with a pencil, mask the monument to prevent the background color from reaching it.

ILLUSTRATIONS FOR REPRODUCTION. The procedure for preparing a monument illustration for reproduction is as follows:

Lay a frisket over the entire drawing. First cut the shaded planes of the monument and air-brush them. To produce marble or granite effects, lay wet sand on a blotter and then sprinkle it on the open areas of the frisket. Then apply a light air-brush spray over the sand. This should be about a value 3 gray. After the color has dried, shift the sand in the area and air-brush again to obtain additional values or tones.

Cut the highlight areas from the frisket and apply an air-brushed wash in a value 3 gray mixture worked from dark to light. Be careful not to over-apply the color on these surfaces. Water marks can be shown by cutting an irregularly shaped card and applying the air-brush color along the edge where desired on the base, pedestal, and other parts of the design.

Cut the background areas in the frisket, piece by piece, working from the background to the foreground and cutting and air-painting the darkest areas first. The background areas should be carefully vignetted into the outer white space.

In the recessed panels in a monument design, a stippled effect is often desired. This is also true of large sand-blasted areas. If the air brush used does not have an adjustment for stippling, the stipple

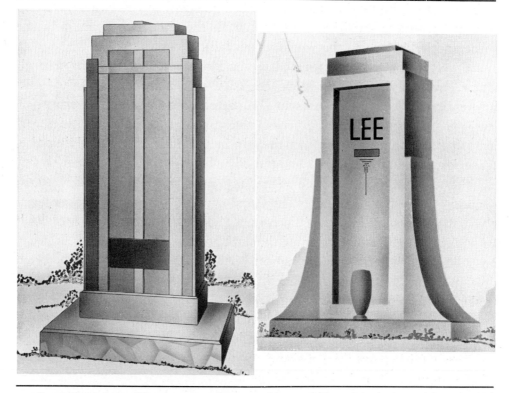

ILLUSTRATIONS FOR REPRODUCTION. Because of its capability of producing subtle tones and blends, giving the rendering of marble and granite a realistic appearance, air-brushed art is most appropriate for making monument illustrations for reproduction.

can be easily obtained by decreasing the amount of air pressure to about eight pounds. The effect can also be achieved by simply squeezing the air-brush hose with one hand.

SYMBOLISM IN MONUMENT DESIGN. If the air-brush artist is to do an amount of monument drawing, he should know something of symbolism in monument design. The vase is the symbol of love, and its treatment varies from the slender type with a simple base to a massive design with a cap and ornamentation. The burning lamp or torch symbolizes immortality, light, and knowledge. The wreath symbolizes memory and friendship. The vine or arch is usually associated with Christianity, and the cross or sacred monogram is regarded as a sign of Christian faith. The ivy leaf represents friendship, and the upright pilaster represents dignity and repose.

PART VII

ARCHITECTURAL DRAWINGS

CHAPTER XXXI

THE ARCHITECTURAL SKETCH

THE ARCHITECTURAL SKETCH is made to illustrate how the exterior or interior of a proposed building will appear after it is constructed. These illustrations are used for all kinds of architectural structures, such as store fronts, business buildings, theatre buildings, industrial buildings, service stations, apartment buildings, and private residences.

Architectural drawings present problems in the representation of various materials with the air brush, such as glass, glass blocks, concrete, cement, brick, granite, marble, sandstone, stainless steel, cast iron, plaster, wood, stone, and slate. The artist should study period molds, cornice construction, door entrances, window molds and details, and period architecture if he is to do very much of this kind of work.

THE SETTING. The architectural sketch consists of two main parts —the structure and the structure's setting or background. The setting around the architectural structure has much to do with the effectiveness of the illustration. It can consist of sky, foliage about the building, and trees, or it can consist of sky and adjoining buildings. If adjoining buildings are to be shown, they should be indicated rather than clearly pictured. Foliage around a building should be in keeping with the building and with the surroundings in which it is to be constructed.

The position of the sun as indicated in the drawing is an all-important factor, as it determines the direction of shades as well as highlights in the drawing. There must be a constancy of shadow direction in drawings of building exteriors. Where artificial illumination is involved in the drawing, the lighting plan should be carefully studied so that correct lighting effects can be accurately shown. Where multiple sources of lighting are involved, multiple shadows often result.

153

THE PROCEDURE. The procedure for making an architectural drawing is as follows:

Make a thumbnail sketch of the subject, selecting an angle that shows the subject to best advantage. The setting should be roughly indicated.

Select a rectangle that will be pleasing in its proportions for the shape of the drawing. Make a drawing of the building with a 2H or 3H pencil. Show all the outstanding lines in proper perspective, and sketch small details free-hand.

Lay vellum masking paper over the entire drawing and cut out small details, such as molds and cornice lines. These should be air-brushed in their natural color unless they are in strong illumination or shade. If they are in strong sunlight, they should be in a color that is a mixture of the natural color and yellow. Portions in shade should first be air-brushed in the natural color and then air-brushed with a gray, the value of which will depend upon the amount of shade. All details around doors, windows, and other shaded parts of a structure should be air-brushed in this way. After these details have been air-

THE ARCHITECTURAL SKETCH. The architectural drawing is unique in that it must present a striking representation at a glance and yet retain clearness of detail. The chief requirement of the drawing is that it present a clear and realistic illustration so that the observer will have no difficulty in visualizing the appearance of the actual structure.

brushed, cut the stencil away from the background and apply the desired colors.

SURFACE REPRESENTATIONS. To indicate bricks in an air-brushed front view of a building, cut a stencil out of celluloid for a group of bricks and spray through the stencil, shifting it to show additional bricks. For an angle view of a brick wall, cut a stencil for the shape and perspective size of bricks nearest to the observer, away from the observer, and in the middle portion of the wall.

Stencils can be likewise cut to indicate slate shingles, wood shingles, and tile. Clapboard can be represented by air-brushing to the straight edge of a piece of cardboard, moving the cardboard along the surface.

Colors should be neutralized in this style of drawing. The tints and shades of the colors should be used rather than the colors themselves in full intensity. Masked portions of the drawing should not be made to appear too harsh. They should stand out and yet blend into the color of the surface indicated.

FREE-HAND SKETCHES. For some subjects, the drawing can be sketched free-hand by drawing the detail lines with a 2H pencil and accenting them with a pencil containing soft lead, which can also be used for drawing the foliage. Then apply the colors with the air brush without the use of stencils to obtain the sky effects, color of the building, and other color desired. Air-painting can be combined with a free-hand drawing in pen and ink to give it a realistic appearance.

Large and pretentious subjects, however, should be carefully delineated in line perspective and just as carefully painted with the air brush. The color adjustment on the air brush should be opened for sky and other wash effects, the tip of the air brush being held several inches from the working surface. Line adjustment on the air brush should be used with the tip held close to the surface for the painting of detail. A drawing that represents a rainy or dark setting can be beautifully painted with the air brush by applying the rainy reflections or dark effects after the rest of the drawing has been completed.

STORE-FRONT DESIGNS. Store-front designs can be ideally executed with the air brush. In air-painting such designs, the part of the building front that is adjacent to the subject portion can be vignetted away. This emphasizes the store front itself and relieves the artist of unnecessary work.

Strong contrast of illumination should be applied in air-painting

STORE-FRONT DESIGNS. Store-front designs can be ideally executed with the air brush.
An effective combination is in the use of hard ink outline and air-brushed treatment.

store-front designs. Two drawings are sometimes made, if interesting
illumination is featured, one showing a daytime view, the other showing
the appearance of the front at night. Always strive for strong effect
in this work.

CHAPTER XXXII

THE SIGN SKETCH

THE PREPARATION of an air-brushed sales drawing or design sketch of an electrical advertising display on a building should include the showing of day and night representations. This is often done by making a broken sketch, the upper or lower portion representing the sign as seen by day, and the other half representing the sign at night. Two complete drawings, one a day view and the other a night view, are sometimes required, in addition to drawings of structural details and combination sketches showing the application of a sign to a particular architectural structure.

SKETCH REQUIREMENTS. The artist should bear in mind several things that should guide him in the work of making pleasing and acceptable electrical advertising design sketches. The sale of the display often depends upon the design sketch, so it must be presented in the most attractive way possible. The design should be shown in harmony with the architecture of the structure to which it is to be applied. Every portion of the design should be absolutely clear, so there will be no questions raised by a prospective sign buyer when the sketch is presented for his consideration.

The lettering of the sign should be clear and sharply defined, and it should be of a style that can be easily and quickly read from a distance. The colors selected should be those that have the utmost of attention value, and yet they should not repeat the colors of other signs in the vicinity or the color of any illumination already present on the structure to receive the sign. The day and night aspects of the sign should be clearly portrayed.

The structure should be indicated, if possible, to show its relation to the proposed display design and aid the prospect in visualizing the display as applied to his business. The prestige of the firm buying the display should be suggested in the design and coloring. Always remember the modern tendency in sign design toward structural beauty, simplicity of line, and the avoidance of over-ornamentation.

THE DAY SKETCH. The careful rendering from the rough design is developed into the finished design. Exact application of lettering and ornament is then developed, and colors are selected for the body of the sign, lighting, and ornament.

AIR BRUSHING THE SKETCH. The best effect can be obtained in air-brushing the body of the sign by confining the darkest tones nearer the outer edge of the design, leaving the middle areas open.

THE DAY SKETCH. The procedure for making the day sketch is first to make a rough sketch in pencil to develop the idea of the design. A careful rendering from this rough design is then developed into the finished design. Exact application of lettering and ornament is then developed, and colors are selected for the body of the sign, lighting, and ornament.

Apply an over-all frisket, made of vellum and cement, to the drawing. Beginning with the small details, such as small letters and outlining, cut the stencil for each part, wipe the cement out of the opening, and apply the desired color. The drawing should be made, of course, on a high grade of illustration board so that the cement does not stain the surface and so the surface is not torn when the frisket is removed.

After air-brushing the details, remove the frisket and apply a new one. This time cut out the body of the sign and air-brush in the design color, leaving the details masked. The order of this procedure can be reversed in some cases where intricate ornament and structure are involved.

THE NIGHT SKETCH. The simplest way to make the night sketch is to trace the day sketch on architectural tracing paper and transfer this tracing to black cardboard. It might be necessary to chalk the back of the tracing paper to obtain a line that can be easily seen on the black card.

The sign can be rendered in a variety of ways. One way is to outline the design with a silver pencil, and to apply the illumination in the colors of each part of the design with a fairly open adjustment of the air brush. The lettering can be applied with an ordinary lettering brush over these illumination lines. This procedure produces the glow about the neon tube letters.

Unusual drawings can be made with the architectural background indicated very lightly in bronze or gold powder. To do this, mask the drawing and cut a stencil for the background. Air-brush the binder for the powder and then apply the powder with an air-brush unit constructed especially for such work. Ready-mixed bronze, gold, and silver paints should be avoided, as these tend to clog the air brush.

PART VIII

PHOTOGRAPH RETOUCHING

CHAPTER XXXIII

RETOUCHING PROCEDURES

THROUGH THE YEARS for more than a generation, the air brush has remained the ideal instrument for the retouching of photographs. This form of art work can be called an art in itself, for expert retouching artists are able to produce some truly remarkable "works of art" in the transformations they create from mediocre photographs.

WHAT RETOUCHING DOES. Purposes of retouching the photograph for reproduction are to remove the defects and unnecessary shadows, and strengthen indistinct parts and the outline of the photograph. Retouching simplifies and strengthens the background, removes the shades that are improper because of poor illumination on the subject, removes unnecessary reflected lights, and simplifies and strengthens the detail involved.

RETOUCHING MATERIALS. The following materials are needed by the air-brush artist who engages in photograph retouching: Surgical cotton swabs, a sensitive air brush, retouching colors, alcohol, a set of ruling pens, inking compass, spinner, bow compass, No. 1 and No. 2 paint brushes, white porcelain tray with eight divisions, several small jars of the three-ounce size, and soft wool cloths, in addition to friskets and other accessories usually required for air-brush work.

COLORS FOR RETOUCHING. The list of colors for retouching should include reproduction white, reproduction black, and reproduction gray, preferably values 3, 6, and 7. To familiarize yourself with the use of these colors, make the value scale with them. This develops ability to mix the exact values before applying them. All opaque colors should be mixed in the exact values in the white porcelain tray before they are applied with the air brush.

USING FRISKETS. A photograph that is rather dark will present outlines of certain parts so indistinctly that when the usual frisket is laid over the photograph, the artist can not see through it sufficiently. Such a photograph requires the use of a cement frisket. This is made of a diluted mixture of rubber cement. A thin coat is applied over the photograph and allowed to dry until it will not pull upward when the point of a pencil is applied to it. Special thinners for various makes of cement are available. The area to be retouched is then cut with a stencil knife along the outlines of the area. The cement between these outlines is rolled back with a flat-edged swab. This operation is repeated until all parts of the photograph have been retouched.

USING SWABS. You will find in retouching photographs that much can be accomplished with the use of swabs in the achieving of intermediate tones. Areas can be air-brushed and then wiped with a swab so that the gray value in the photograph will show through. The work will be greatly facilitated by keeping on hand a variety of these swabs

PHOTOGRAPH RETOUCHING. Through the years for more than a generation, the air brush has remained the ideal instrument for the retouching of photographs.

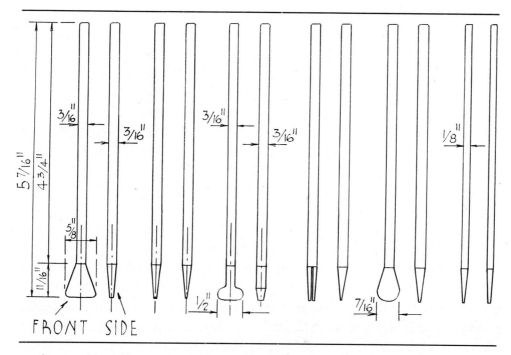

FRONT   SIDE

SWABS. Retouching work will be greatly facilitated by keeping on hand a variety of swabs in different shapes, made by placing surgical cotton on ends of brush handles and orange sticks.

in different shapes, made by placing surgical cotton on ends of brush handles and orange sticks.

ILLUMINATION. The art of photograph retouching requires serious study of the different kinds of illumination. If a definite condition of illumination is not apparent in a given photograph, assume that the lighting of the subject or subjects is conventional lighting. If there is, however, part of the photograph that is correct and that does not need retouching and if the portion has clearly shown the light direction, then that light direction must be followed in retouching the rest of the photograph. If more than one source of illumination are used, follow the direction of the source that seems to be the strongest. If there is light from the left and light from the right and if the illumination from the right is stronger, then the light direction to use is the one supplied by the illumination from the right.

ILLUMINATION CLASSIFIED. Illumination of the photographed subject may be classified as (1) conventional, (2) spot, (3) diffused, and (4) uniform. If a photograph shows gray tones of nearly the same value in the different parts, make some of these parts light and some dark to create strong contrast. Strong contrast is necessary for the production of clear half-tone reproductions. The amount of contrast in the retouched photograph should vary directly with the fineness of the half-tone screen that is to be used in reproducing the photograph. Contrast in a retouched photograph for reproduction in newspapers must be stronger than the contrast for reproduction in a catalog, since a coarser half-tone screen is used for the newspaper half-tone.

TECHNICAL AND MECHANICAL SUBJECTS. The most difficult photographs to retouch are those involving technical and mechanical subjects with which the artist is often not entirely familiar. This information regarding points to be observed in the original photograph should therefore be helpful toward attaining desirable results.

Interiors of factories lose much in detail because of perspective and illumination in the background portion. Decide how much this needs to be strengthened to bring it forward and give it sufficient emphasis.

Observe if the different kinds of metals shown are brought out by the gray tones in the photograph. If not, the values for the different kinds of metal must be applied to them in retouching.

Observe scratches or flaws on the photograph and retouch them. If they are not retouched, they are liable to show on the reproduction, particularly when a half-tone of fine screen is used.

Floor coverings in unretouched photographs of factory interiors do not usually present a clean, smooth appearance. Retouch these in flat tones. Needless detail in the picture should be eliminated. Objects such as old gloves, overalls, scraps, and the like should be air-brushed out of the picture.

The grain of wood on wooden objects is often weak and needs to be strengthened. If there are adjoining steel parts that appear in the same tone, making their outlines indistinct, decide which of these should be light and which dark to give clarity.

Study the gears in a machine-parts photograph to see if the outlines of the teeth are sufficiently sharp. Study the grooves and ridges on the machine parts to see if their shaded sides give sufficient indication of depth. Study slots cut in face plates and in the end bells of motors to ascertain if sufficient depth is shown. Observe the shapes of nuts and bolts to determine if the shades on them are correct for their forms.

CHAPTER XXXIV

RETOUCHING PROBLEMS

SINCE MUCH can be learned simply by studying actual examples typical of the retouching problems an artist can expect to encounter, we shall here consider some of those problems. Study of these procedures, in addition to actual practice, can aid largely in giving a good general knowledge of retouching work.

RETOUCHING THE SHOE PICTURE. One of the commonest retouching tasks that comes into the average studio is that of retouching photographs of shoes, usually for illustrations in catalogs and in publication advertisements. First make a study of the actual texture of the leather, details of the vamp, the stitching, lacing, and all other details.

The problem of retouching is largely that of strengthening and correcting the photograph and of adding a few touches to emphasize the texture of the material and bring out the details of the parts. There is almost a constancy of highlight shape and direction on the basic parts of the shoe, such as the heel and vamp, since there is very little fundamental change in shape. In other words, the shoe must follow the contour and form of the foot.

The original photograph itself can be retouched, but if it is extremely weak, an enlargement or tracing should be made from the photograph. The enlargement will make the work much easier. If a tracing is used, however, it will have to be transferred to illustration board. It is then ready to be treated as an air-brushed drawing.

Retouching a photograph of a shoe involves the following: The elimination of improper illumination on the shoe; applying highlights on the vamp and heel; masking with a frisket, if necessary, the ribbons, cut-out areas, bows, and other details; repeated air-brushing, if necessary, using special celluloid cut-out shapes to produce leather texture; outlining of indistinct areas, such as the sole and heel; separating with a different shade of gray the areas of different colors in two-tone shoes.

RETOUCHING THE COSTUMED FIGURE. Surrounding objects often cast a shadow across part of the costumed figure and destroy the clear-

A RETOUCHED SHOE PICTURE. The problem of retouching the shoe picture is largely that of strengthening and correcting the photograph and of adding a few touches to emphasize the texture of the material and bring out details of the parts.

ness of that part. If a man is wearing a dark gray suit the shadow cast across one arm might make that arm appear practically black.

The first step in retouching this arm is to lay a frisket over the arm area and cut a stencil for it. The next step is to judge the value of the shade areas upon the portion of the costume that is correctly illuminated and to mix that value in reproduction colors. This value is then applied to the sleeve area along the shaded portion. The normal value of the suit is then applied over the illuminated portion. The extreme darks in the creases of the sleeve are obtained by using a swab and wiping out part of the color so that the dark photograph will show through. This will produce sharp accents in the creases and folds. Necessary highlights can then be air-brushed with reproduction white in a fine spray.

CONFLICTING ILLUMINATION. The following is the procedure for retouching a photograph where the conflicting illumination sets up distorted shades and shadow areas on the objects in the photograph:

Determine the single source of illumination by careful study of the lights and shades on the foreground. Using this source as the standard for illumination, plan the value range upon the foreground objects. Apply a frisket over the entire photograph and cut the stencil for the parts of the foreground objects that need to be retouched according to the value range planned from this single source of illumination.

Cut the stencil for the background area and vignette the background according to the required strength of the outlines of the parts of the composition. Cut the stencils for the parts that need to be eliminated entirely. Air-brush these in the value which will obliterate them.

Cut the stencil for the parts illuminated by the other light sources and shade these according to the illumination from the one light source selected. Apply the necessary outline with retouch brushes to strengthen the drawing.

DIFFUSED LIGHTING. The following procedure is for retouching a photograph taken when the subject was in diffused lighting:

Select the area to be outstanding and ascertain the value range upon its parts. Lay a frisket over the photograph by putting a few spots of rubber cement in the needed places and laying a sheet of frisket paper over the photograph. Using a stiff card with a straight edge and working from the center of the frisket paper, draw the cement out evenly beneath the frisket. Take great care in doing this to be sure that all air bubbles are removed from beneath the frisket paper. Cut the frisket for the principal element of the photographic composition.

Mix a value range of grays from light to dark. This value range must be in keeping with the amount of reduction to which the photograph is to be subjected and with the kind of paper upon which the reproduction plate will be printed. Lay in these colors with the air brush, working from light to dark.

Plan the value range for the surrounding parts so that each part will stand out and yet contrast to some extent with the principal element of the composition. Outline with reproduction white all portions that need to be strengthened. Air-brush secondary parts where needed. Add the darker outlines with a paint brush. Change the value of the background to contrast, if possible, with the other elements in the subject. Check the drawing to see if there is an indication of light direction and a constancy of this direction.

RETOUCHING OF LETTERING. Lettering that has to be retouched generally comes under one of the following classifications:

Lettering which is partially obliterated by shadows cast by another object; lettering that fades into the background; lettering that because of the shape of the object is partially shaded; lettering with outlines made indistinct by reflected lights; lettering distorted by the photographic process to the point that it is illegible; lettering with outlines that are hazy because the color around the lettering photographed is nearly the same value as the lettering itself; lettering made indistinct by perspective distortion.

Where lettering has been partially obliterated by an object, it is necessary to lay a frisket over the lettering and cut a stencil for it. The value of gray desired for the lettering is then applied to the stencil.

Lettering made indistinct by perspective distortion will often require the air-brushing of the area upon which the distorted lettering exists, in the value desired for that area. Lay a frisket over the area and lay off upon this frisket the undistorted lettering. Cut the stencil for this lettering and air-brush it in the value desired for the lettering.

Where lettering is partially shaded by the form of an object the procedure is to lay a frisket over the lettering and cut out the stencil for it. Where the form of an object has darkened the lettering simply air-brush these letters with a lighter value. Where object color has photographed light, air-brush around the lettering with a darker gray. If the object is actually light and the lettering dark, lay a frisket over the lettering and cut the frisket away from the lettering, leaving the frisket paper over the lettering itself. Air-brush around this lettering with the gray desired. Remove the frisket and rubber cement, and retouch the edges of the letters with a small brush or pen.

A Simple Problem. Illumination in many photographs is such that the clearness of the objects is lost. Here are "before and after" views of a photograph retouched to improve the appearance of the floor and background, and to correct the uneven lighting that puts the right side of the object in darkness.

Lettering made indistinct by reflected lights often requires the retouching of both the lettering and the area around it. If these reflected lights are very strong, lay a frisket over the lettering, cutting out the portion around the lettering. Air-brush in a gray tone that will remove the reflections. After this retouching is dry, retouch the lettering itself to remove the white spots or other reflected illumination defects.

In retouching of lettering, the artist should exercise a tremendous amount of common sense. Distorted lettering can often be saved by retouching one or two letters. This may consist of simply changing their widths, part of their form, or their spacing. It may consist of a little shaded outline.

NEGATIVE RETOUCHING. Blemishes, weak outlines, and surfaces whose values are incorrect may be rectified by retouching directly upon the negative. This retouching can be accomplished in several different ways. The first method is to use an ordinary opaque solution in the air brush, putting in small details with fine adjustment and treating the larger areas with an open adjustment of the air brush. In retouching directly upon a negative, an extremely sensitive type of air brush should be used when no stencils are employed.

In working upon a negative, a light-box or a tracing table is required. A simple tracing table can be made by constructing a frame of 1-by-3-inch white pine, 18 inches wide and 24 inches long. Into this frame should be fitted, in picture-frame style, a ¼-inch piece of plate glass. Underneath this frame at each end of it should be placed two lights. When the negative is placed on top of the plate glass over these lights the details can be clearly seen.

Clear celluloid film can be laid over the negative and scratched with a knife point to outline the parts that need to be protected by a stencil. This clear sheet of celluloid can then be placed upon the drawing board and the stencil cut out. Stencils can also be made of vellum paper and simply held in place during the air brushing.

Another method of retouching the negative is to spray retouching fluid over the negative with an air brush and then apply the desired retouching with a retouch pencil. Novel effects can be obtained by using a stipple effect with the air brush. Opaquing solutions may be used for this stipple. Another treatment is to apply the retouch fluid with a stipple effect, and then shade over this lightly with a retouch pencil. This will produce a soft, graded stipple effect.

CHAPTER XXXV

TINTING PROCEDURES

PHOTOGRAPH TINTING with the air brush is a branch of re-touching art that applies to photographs, photographic enlargements, and photo murals used for purposes other than reproduction. The tinting is usually done to give natural colors to the photograph instead of retouching it in grays as for reproduction.

TINTING COLORS. A photograph may be tinted with a solution of prepared water colors or oil paints made for that purpose. Before beginning any tinting work with oil washes, practice making value scales with the oil colors. Marvelous effects can be produced with little practice by blending one color into another in the tinting procedure. Mixing of colors ought to be avoided as much as possible because of their tendency to separate.

APPLYING COLORS. Use an air brush that produces a fine spray when applying the tinting colors. Apply the color washes first to the large areas, such as the cheek and neck if the photograph is a portrait, and then to the small areas. When air-brushing the large areas, hold the air brush several inches from the working surface.

THE PHOTO MURAL. The photo mural is made from a photographic enlargement. The enlargement should be neither extremely light or extremely dark for tinting purposes. An enlargement that is extremely dark neutralizes the air-brush colors to the point that color tinting is extremely difficult. The colors are applied to the enlargement to beautify it, increase the effect of the third dimension, and to make the photograph more realistic in appearance.

A PRODUCTION SET-UP. A production set-up for tinting the popular photo mural would involve a line of tables and an air line. The tables should be opposite large racks upon which would be mounted the photo murals to be tinted. Each artist should have a pressure regulator and gauge connected to his particular outlet. The spacing between the tables should be about 10 feet in order to accommodate the larger murals.

One man should specialize in open effects, such as skies and large foreground and background areas. Another should specialize in the tinting of representations that requires ability in handling detail. A third man should handle the extremely small detail. Other members of the department can include mounters, a frisket cutter, and an artist skilled in brush retouching by hand.

HANDLING COLORS. Select a good brand of dye colors or alcohol-solvent colors for the tinting of the photo mural. It is extremely convenient to have a supply of three-ounce color jars, one to hold each of the different colors, and thus avoid washing and refilling a single color cup. Tube water colors can be used if the enlargement is not to be exposed to moisture.

Apply the background color first, using a frisket to cover the other parts only when absolutely necessary. If possible, start with the warm colors, such as yellow, red, and yellow-green, and work into cool colors of the composition. It is sometimes desirable to apply the yellows first and work the blues over them to make use of the transparency of the colors.

THE LANDSCAPE SCENE. In tinting the photo mural of a landscape scene, for example, where background foliage is part of the picture, it should be air-brushed in large masses. Foreground foliage in which leaf contour is plainly discernible should be applied with a closed adjustment of the air-brush tip. In air-brushing foliage shown in sunlight, it should be remembered that the sunlight strikes the upper and outer areas. These should be in a pale yellow "sunshine" tint and the greens and blues and blue-greens should then be applied in order toward the shaded side of the foliage.

The sky in the landscape scene becomes lighter toward the horizon, so begin at the top of the sky portion and work downward toward the horizon line, moving the air brush away from the working surface as it is moved downward, to insure the gradual lightening of values. The darks in the photograph should be tapered with the darker tones of the colors. The darks of the photograph neutralize all brown shades, consequently the amount of red and yellow in the browns should be increased to offset this neutralization. In other words, it is necessary to work in a decided red-brown or yellow-brown to offset the dark grays of the photograph.

PART IX

THE MURAL

CHAPTER XXXVI

PLANNING THE MURAL

MURAL PAINTING has taken on a new significance generally since the sponsorship by the federal government of this form of art decoration for public buildings. The mural is now seen in cafes, hotel lobbies, theatres, private clubs, office building lobbies, and even in private homes and apartment buildings. The growth of the use of murals has naturally opened new sources of earnings for the air-brush artist.

THE MURAL IN AIR-BRUSH. The air-brush medium of painting lends itself toward the modern abstraction and stylized form of composition so popular in the modern mural, as well as for the mural in the more conventional style. Air-brush art, because of its flexibility, lends itself to all techniques of painting. In mural painting it offers many possibilities when combined with other painting methods.

Subjects for murals cover a wide range and variety. Political and social movements are portrayed in some, while other subjects are strongly influenced by regional ideas of social, scenic, industrial, or historical nature.

KINDS OF MURALS. We might classify murals from a practical standpoint as being (1) removable wall panels, (2) fixed panels, (3) photographic murals, (4) frescos, and (5) relief representations. From the standpoint of air-brush rendering, we are concerned chiefly with the first three of these.

REMOVABLE PANELS. Murals that are of the removable-panel type are generally painted on canvas or a special grade of composition wood with a surface treated for that purpose. Plywood panels may be used if the surface is carefully primed and treated.

Canvas is available in widths of 36, 41, 42, and 54 inches. The texture of the canvas is a matter of individual choice, but smooth sur-

REMOVABLE PANEL. Murals of the removable-panel type are generally painted on canvas or a special grade of composition wood with a surface treated for that purpose. Plywood panels may be used if the surface is carefully primed and treated. This decorative panel was air-painted in oil colors.

faces are more suitable for air-brushed techniques, especially if the subject matter involves much fine detail.

When a large mural is to be air-painted, the widths of canvas should be joined and cemented before color is applied. Seams must be carefully made to prevent them from showing prominently when color is applied over them with the air brush. It is best to use composition wood instead of canvas for especially wide murals, as the joints are then easier to hide.

An excellent surface can be obtained by gluing the wood panels and cutting them to size and then instead of painting on them, use them for a base upon which the canvas can be cemented. The best air-brushed results will be obtained by using the primed canvas. In this way, the work can be done directly on the surface, which lends itself to the more carefully made detailed line drawing necessary in air-brush work. Otherwise, a thin coat of varnish evenly applied will be necessary to prime the surface.

Over-priming of the canvas should be avoided, and the priming should be applied as uniformly as possible to eliminate the hazard of staining when the air-brush color is applied to the primed surface. Varnish should be applied to the surface with a touch-up air brush. It is well to make test samples of the canvas before the actual priming is started.

Canvas can be primed with a mixture of flat white and varnish for large-scale work. The primer should be applied as evenly as possible, however, so that there will be no "soft spots" on the canvas.

LARGE FIXED PANELS. A mural painted directly upon a wall necessitates the application of a careful priming to the wall. A plastered wall needs to be filled with a plaster primer and then finished with a good grade of varnish.

Scaffolding for the artist in painting large wall murals is usually built of 2-by-4 and 1-by-12 lumber. Scaffolding is costly on a large mural, and the artist should previously obtain an estimate of the cost for its construction so that he can include it in his own estimate. The ladder-and-plank arrangement can be used for small murals.

SMALL FIXED PANELS. Small murals applied directly to walls already painted usually fall into two classes. One class is the conventionalized design that makes use of the wall color, which will show through the parts of the design. The other class is the mural that is to cover the wall that has already been painted. In either case the wall must be carefully cleaned to remove all grease and dirt, and all cracks must be filled and retouched.

PLANNING THE MURAL DESIGN. In planning an original sketch for a mural, the artist is confronted with problems that are in many respects similar to those encountered in the designing of twenty-four-

PLANNING THE MURAL DESIGN. In planning an original sketch for a mural, the artist is confronted with problems that are in many respects similar to those encountered in the designing of twenty-four-sheet posters. This is a rough crayon sketch of a mural preliminary to airbrushing.

sheet posters. First, he must realize that extremely small detail is lost at the distances from which the mural is best observed.

The next consideration that must be kept in mind is the effect of the enlargement of color areas. Those that appear of the right strength in the small-scale sketch will often appear to be too strong in the enlargement. Cool colors, particularly the blue-grays and blue-greens, have greater powers in neutralizing the warm colors surrounding them when they are enlarged, so they, too, must be used with skill.

When planning the original design for a mural, a careful study should be made of the illumination of the building in which the mural is to be placed. The direction of light on the proposed area for the mural should be considered from the standpoint of illumination.

Colors of the walls and the surrounding objects in the interior should also be considered, as the colors in the mural must not clash with the surroundings. Since the mural is a thing to be "lived with," its colors must be such that they do not fatigue, but are always interesting. For this reason, the color values and chromas should be held down to a lower key than is the practice in ordinary painting.

THE COMPOSITION. The story told by the mural must be obvious. The theme must be well-defined and strongly revealed in a well-knit composition. The center of interest in the mural must be concentrated in most cases slightly above the geometric center and along the vertical center line or slightly below the geometric center and along the vertical center line of the area.

If human figures are involved in the composition, one figure must dominate. The mural must portray action and be vital in its composition and yet retain something of a conventionalized treatment. Care must be used in making the layout of a mural involving figures, to be sure that the features in the faces of the principal figures are large enough and clear enough so that when the mural is viewed from a distance the features will be clearly perceived.

Fidelity to details must be maintained in mural composition when the theme is of historical or regional nature. Considering that murals remain in a place for a period of years during which styles of dress are changed, figures in symbolic compositions should be draped so that no particular period of time is represented by the mode of dress. This is difficult to do and requires preliminary practice in making many detailed drape studies before the finished sketch of the mural is attempted.

CHAPTER XXXVII

AIR-PAINTING THE MURAL

THE ORIGINAL SKETCH for a mural is usually prepared as a line drawing, and a section through this drawing is then rendered in full color. The beginner in mural work should complete the coloring of the original drawing and have the colors checked from the standpoint of balance, harmony, rhythm, and color emphasis. Make careful observations as to the closeness of hues and chromas. If necessary, make side drawings of value scales of these colors. Above everything else, visualize each color area as magnified to the scale of the mural, and make the drawing in scale for projection to the desired size.

THE DETAILED SKETCH. The original sketch for a mural is usually prepared as a line drawing, and a section through this drawing is then rendered in full color. The beginner in mural work, however, should complete the coloring of the original drawing and have the colors checked from the standpoint of balance, harmony, rhythm, and emphasis.

THE DETAILED STUDIES. After the original sketch has been prepared and approved, prepare detailed studies of the hands, feet, and
heads of the figures in the composition. These should be separate
analytical drawings. Also make detailed drawings of the forms of
any parts with which you are not familiar. This is especially true in
the painting of technical subjects. Then correct the original sketch with
the aid of the analytical detailed studies.

PROJECTING THE SKETCH. Project the drawing onto white or
brown paper, and then trace its outlines with a tracing wheel. The
drawing is then ready for pouncing onto the mural surface. Charcoal
dust or scenic colors may be used for pouncing and a pouncing bag can
be made of cheesecloth or organdy.

AIR-PAINTING EQUIPMENT. When the pattern is applied to the
surface, you are ready to begin the actual air-brushing. For this, you
will need an extra long air-brush hose, a portable compressor, an air
brush with a round-headed nozzle, several three-ounce color jars, and
several air-brush tips.

Work that is extremely large requires the use of a touch-up air
brush and an air compressor capable of producing seventy-five pounds
of air. On these large murals, the heavier type of ground oil color
must be used, consequently the air pressure must be increased. The
artist's type of air brush, however, can be used for applying the details
in the painting.

PREPARING COLOR. Use a good grade of studio tube color for all
detail parts. Ground oil colors of the same manufacture may be used
for the larger expanses in the mural area. Mix the colors carefully
and thin them with a good grade of medicinal turpentine. A good
thinning mixture for this purpose is three parts of linseed oil and five
parts of turpentine. Keep these colors in jars with tops so that no
dust particles can reach them. They must be thoroughly stirred and
strained through organdy before being placed in the color cups.

APPLYING COLOR. Begin with the large areas first and air-brush
them with a large fan spray. This covers the areas uniformly and
quickly. The blending of color into the detail areas can be easily done
and the proper colors applied to those areas. The best results can be
obtained by allowing each color to dry before the next color is applied
over it. Clearer tones result from this procedure.

Use extreme care to avoid over-modeling one part of the composition and treating the other parts with too few values or with a poster treatment. There should be consistency in the value ranges and in the handling of all parts of the composition. A careful analysis of each of the objects into the basic geometric forms and the subsequent application of the theory of shading of these forms will aid materially in giving uniform treatment to the elements in the composition.

Where many straight lines are involved, use long strips of cardboard or stencil board to produce them. Shapes of the same size that are to be repeated can also be cut out of stencil board and held in place for air-brushing. Arcs and long sweeping curves can be executed with the aid of previously cut-out masks held in place while the color is being applied. For large murals, wall board can be cut with a cutting machine to form partial masks for air-brushing special designs, rules, and curved shapes.

The reflected color of one object upon another should be carefully studied. This reflected color is easily applied by simply blending the reflected color into the original color of the object upon whose surface it is reflected. Likewise, a careful study should be made of the shadow formation of each object with reference to the illumination of the painting. When these shadows are applied, the value impression desired for the entire painting should be kept in mind.

UTILIZING WALL COLOR. When working on a wall whose color will serve as part of the design, be extremely careful that the friskets are kept clean and that no mistakes are made in color application, as it is difficult to match the wall color. A carefully planned drawing carefully air-brushed will prevent this difficulty.

With such designs, keep the color scheme extremely simple, as, for example, a black design on a buff-colored wall, a dark green design on a light green wall, black or dark brown on a cream wall, a dark red design on a light brown wall, light blue or light green on a white wall.

These paintings can often be applied entirely with the aid of friskets previously prepared. The frisket paper or stencil board must be stiff enough to retain its shape when cut into these large areas. If friskets are used for applying the design, a pounce pattern will not be required. The design can be projected directly onto the stencil board. For the projection, a machine whose lens is accurately ground will be required to prevent distortion.

COVERING AN OLD SURFACE. When the wall painting is to cover

an old surface, prime the wall after it has been cleaned. This priming should consist of two coats of flat white followed by a coat of thin varnish. A pounce pattern cut for the design is pounced on the wall in the usual manner.

On small murals with small background areas, begin with the figures and work outward, making the necessary adjustments in the background colors as you proceed. If the wall has been improperly painted, the old paint should be partially or entirely removed before priming is applied.

Wooden walls that have not been painted require that the area for the mural should be carefully sanded and then treated with a good grade of wood filler. Soft woods require at least two coats of this filler, sanded with No. 1 and No. 00 sandpaper between the coats. Over this, apply clear varnish or a coat of flat white followed by thin varnish. Be extremely careful in the preparation of this surface. Where the wood has been previously painted, it should be scraped, sanded, and then varnished lightly.

ACHIEVING BEAUTIFUL CREATIONS. The air brush affords a great variety of soft, intermediate tones that can be beautifully utilized on large-scale mural work. Beautiful renderings can be made with the primary colors of red, yellow, and blue, and the binary colors of orange, green, and purple, and by blending these colors over one another to produce intermediate colors. However, when beginning the work, plan and mix all required colors individually.

The air-brushed work can be combined with ordinary painting methods to good advantage. The mural can be painted as usual, and the air brush used for sky effects or large backgrounds. It is necessary to mask the area painted by hand while the background or sky area is being air-painted. Fog effects, cloudiness, and rain can be air-brushed over an ordinary painting to produce realistic effects.

Attractive pictorial murals are created by painting the foreground in full color by hand, and by air-brushing the middle ground and sky. The sky can be air-brushed to produce cloud effects of untold beauty. The cloud outline should be faintly marked on the surface. Beginning with a blue at the top, work downward and around the cloud areas. At the base of the clouds, blue-gray should be applied. White should be atomized into the cloud areas, followed by the desired reflected colors, such as red or yellow in the form of streaks.

PART X

FLOCKING WITH THE AIR BRUSH

CHAPTER XXXVIII

AIR-BRUSHED FLOCK

FLOCKING with the air brush is an easy method of applying flock in the creation of beautiful cloth-like surfaces to produce decorations, advertising displays, and for coating or decorating many objects. Flock is a by-product of wool, cotton, silk, and rayon. It is cut to various degrees of fineness, and it is produced in a variety of colors. It is available in lengths of 1/64, 1/16, and 1/8 inch. It can be applied with a special flocking air brush over a damp binder or sizing previously applied to a surface with an air brush through a stencil, with screen-process printing, or by other methods.

KINDS OF FLOCK. Flock is available in colors of bleached white, orange mineral, gold, silver, black, emerald green, medium blue, medium chrome yellow, bright red, magenta shades, cream colors, dark brown, and light brown. These colors can be mixed together prior to their application to provide intermediate hues, if desired. Beautiful effects can be obtained by blending flock of one color into another in the air-brushing application.

The artist working with flock should obtain samples of the different kinds of flock so that he can select the kind—such as wool, rayon, silk, or cotton—that is best suited to his needs. He should become acquainted, for example, with the silky appearance of the long flock, such as the 1/8-inch rayon, and with the suede-like appearance of the 1/64-inch length.

EQUIPMENT FOR FLOCKING. The equipment required for flocking with the air brush depends upon the method of application used. It is well, however, to be equipped for the two most-used methods of applying the flock binder—the air-brush method and the screen-process method.

Such equipment includes an air brush for applying binder, an air brush for applying flock, screen-process equipment, stencils and accessories for use with the air brush, flock binders, thinner for binders, an assortment of flock, a stiff brush, soft cloths, pans and trays for collecting unused flock, a portable air compressor capable of developing up to seventy-five pounds of air, a respirator, and goggles.

AIR BRUSHES FOR FLOCKING. An air brush is especially made for the applying of flock, dry powders, and material in granular form. It is efficient in operation, and delivers the flock in a round or wide fan spray. The use of this equipment has simplified the applying of the flock, which was formerly sifted or sprinkled evenly on the receiving surface, usually by means of a sifter-like device that was agitated over the surface.

A special type of air brush is also available for the applying of heavy liquids, such as binders made exclusively for flocking, and of paints, lacquers, sizings, enamels, light-bodied synthetics, and other painting and finishing materials of like consistency.

THE FLOCKING BOOTH. If a great deal of flocking is done, a small room or booth is necessary. It can be constructed chiefly of wall board or composition board, and should be provided with a ventilating system that will meet requirements of local health laws. Air-brush and spray-gun manufacturers can furnish ready-made booths for this purpose. A respirator and goggles should be worn by the artist when applying the flock, as constant working with flock without such protection is injurious to health.

STENCILS. Flocking with the air brush is done through stencils. The stencil for use in applying the flock can be made of vellum paper, stencil board, or brown wrapping paper and cut with a stencil knife according to the design to be flocked. The stencil is pinned in place or fastened with masking tape or rubber cement, depending upon the kind of surface to which the flock is to be applied. If the surface is cloth, the stencil can be pinned or thumb-tacked in place.

When the flock is to be applied to a quantity of designs that are all the same, the screen-process stencil method is used to apply the binder to the surface. The hand-cut film-paper stencil is very adaptable for this purpose.

BINDERS FOR FLOCKING. Binder or sizing for flock can be applied with an air brush suitable for the purpose, or with the screen process, wood cuts, wood blocks, linoleum cuts, or with a brush by hand. When it is applied with the air brush, the air pressure must vary according to the consistency and kind of binder used. Light-grade lacquers, when used as binders, can be atomized with as little as thirty-five pounds of air, while some of the heavier binders require forty-five and fifty pounds of air.

With the development of binders made especially for flocking, it is possible to use flock with ease for various treatments. These binders are a form of delayed-drying lacquer. One type of binder is applied with the air brush and requires the use of stencils, and another type can be applied to matte and cloth surfaces with a hand brush, making unnecessary the use of stencils.

Shellac can be used as a binder where the work is to be of a temporary nature and where there is no need for flexibility of the surface material after the flock has been applied. The covering of display pieces not to be subjected to a great deal of wear can be flocked on a shellac binder.

The binder for applying flock to cloth should be one that is flexible when it is flocked and dried, otherwise the flock will not be permanent. There are several commercial binders available that possess this quality of flexibility. One, for example, is especially suitable for paper and cardboard. It is white and can be made the same color as the flock to be used by simply adding a small amount of tube color. In this way, the binder and the flock can be made to match. When flock is applied to cloth that is to be washed or dry-cleaned, the binder used must be one that will withstand such treatments.

In air-brushing the binder, the air brush should not be held very long on one portion of the design, but it should be fanned over the entire area. This should be repeated until the open areas in the stencil feel tacky to the touch.

FLOCKING APPLICATIONS

CHAPTER XXXIX

THE AIR-BRUSH ARTIST can realize the many possibilities in flocking with the air brush only when he begins to experiment with some of the many uses of flock. How he can take advantage of all the possibilities awaiting him depends only upon his creative ability and his ingenuity in making the most of each possiblity.

Uses of Flock. Flock has been used for years in the upholstering of furniture, in the making of wall paper, pennants, banners, and for other purposes. Its use has extended to include wall tapestries, wall hangings, display backgrounds, display fixtures and forms, display cards, interior signs, advertising novelties, valances, mirror backs, wall decorations, finishes for cabinet interiors, athletic goods, and many other applications.

Air Pressures. In air-brushing flock, the air pressure should be made to vary slightly according to the kind of material to which the flock is being applied. The flock can be driven into the binder sufficiently on a metal surface if a pressure of only thirty-five pounds of air is used on the flock gun. When applying flock to duvetyn or felt. it is best to use about fifty-five pounds of air pressure, while for velour, forty-five pounds of air pressure is ideal.

The length of the flock also has a bearing on the amount of air pressure to be used. Short-length flock, such as the 1/64 inch, can be applied at a slightly lower air pressure than longer flock, such as 1/16 or 1/8 inch. Variation in the air pressure when applying flock of a certain length will cause a slight change in the appearance of the flocked surface.

Pennants. Simple applications of flock are in the making of low-cost pennants on which the lettering or design is flocked with the air brush instead of being first cut out of felt and then sewn or glued onto the background. A procedure for making a small quantity of pennants is as follows: Make a sketch of the lettering for the stencils. Outline the shape of the pennant with pointed chalk on the felt to be used, and cut around the outline with the cutting machine.   Several pennants can be cut at one time.

Pin one of the stencils in place over one of the pennants, which should be in vertical position, and air-brush the flock binder over the open portions of the stencil with the binder applicator.   The amount of binder required can be ascertained by simply touching the open part of the stencil.   If the binder feels tacky or sticky to the touch, a sufficient amount has been applied.

Next air-brush the flock with the flocking unit, working with an air pressure of about fifty pounds, and apply the flock evenly.   The pennant should still be in a vertical position, and provision should be made to catch and collect the excess flock that falls from the stencil. This excess flock can be used again.

The adjustment of the flow of flock must be such that a minimum amount of the flock is emitted at high speed.   This insures the making of a smooth covering, and provides better control of the application.

FLOCKING FOR DISPLAY. This flocked display was in keeping with the product it advertised. Flocking for display provides an attention-getting treatment that gives the observer a most favorable impression.

Let the flock dry for thirty or forty minutes before lifting the stencil, depending upon the kind of binder used. Brush over the flocked design to remove loose flock, and the pennant is completed, except for the adding of tie strips, which are usually sewn to the pennant.

In the making of large quantities of pennants, apply the binder with the screen process stencil. The flocking is then done in the manner just described, each pennant being air-brushed individually as soon as it is screen-processed. This work is best handled by at least two operators—one to do the processing, the other to do the flocking.

BANNERS. There is occasionally a demand for a few large banners that can be easily produced by flocking. In flocking such large pieces, the stencils can be made in sections and the binder and flock applied to a section at a time unless there are several operators.

Beautiful banners can be produced by using a background of white felt and flocking the design and lettering in several different colors of flock. Striking banners can be made on black felt to which gold or silver flock is applied.

ATHLETIC GARMENTS. When applying flocked letters, numerals, or designs to athletic garments, special tables and jigs are used to hold the garment. One company that specializes in the applying of flocked numerals to athletic sweaters has a series of stencil screens, one for each numeral. A special base holds the garment in position. Two arms are hinged at the back of the table and the screen frame with the numeral stencil is inserted between the ends of these arms. By shifting the garment and using these stock numerals, any series of numerals can be easily applied. After the binder has been screen-processed in place, the flock is air-brushed on it. The most economical method of flocking a limited number of garments is to cut a stencil out of stencil board and air-brush the binder through this stencil.

FLOCKING FOR DISPLAY. Decorative and surface effects in flock can be easily applied to window display background panels, display cards, interior signs, cut-outs, show-window floors, walls, display fixtures, and other display accessories. Displays are reflecting more and more the modern trends in design, and the use of flock gives pleasing effects in modern treatments.

There are tremendous possibilities in using three-dimensional display pieces constructed of wood, composition board, or wall board. Parts of these display units can be coated with contrasting colors of

DISPLAY PIECES. When the window is considered as a three-dimensional design rather than two-dimensional, the application of flock ceases to be limited to the window display panel and background, but becomes a vital part of the three-dimensional design of the window as a whole.

flock, which gives them the appearance of being cloth-covered with a soft material.

FLOCKING SUGGESTIONS. The following suggestions will be found helpful in flocking with the air brush:

In applying binder to lettering, it is best to spray more binder around the edges of the letter outlines than in the centers of the letter parts.

You can flock over flock without first removing the initial coating. The only requisite is that the stencils should be held tightly in place while air-brushing the binder in the second application.

When flocking on cloth with a strong nap, the binder should be applied evenly. It should be heavy enough to penetrate into the material.

CONCLUSION

CHAPTER XL

EARNING MONEY WITH THE AIR BRUSH

A QUESTION that is often asked by the student of air-brush art is, "Why should I study air-brush painting?" The answer to this simple question is quite obvious. The artist seeks accomplishment in air-brush art to earn money and to earn it in a variety of ways. The material in this book is in itself suggestive of numerous forms of art work in which the accomplished air-brush artist can earn money with his air brush. This is done in two ways. One is by working independently as a free-lance artist. The other is by working in a salaried position as a staff artist who specializes in air-brush work.

FREE-LANCE WORK. The greatest difficulty in working as a free-lance artist is to get a start. It is no easy matter for an artist to set forth in this work, and the temptation to become discouraged is often permitted to overcome the zeal to establish contacts and to acquaint buyers of art work with his ability. Much of the free-lance artist's success depends upon his efforts to make himself known and to make known the quality of work he is able to produce. This calls for personal contacts and advertising.

Free-lance artists usually have one or more accounts upon which they depend for the greater part of their income. Some obtain these accounts before and some after they set up their free-lance service. The latter course is naturally the more difficult.

The suggestions that follow might be helpful to the free-lance artist in selling his services. Some of these suggestions lead to sources from which the artist can derive constant revenue for his work. These are in addition to the sources of advertising art business, of which there are many in every city.

Air-painting of portraits offers a good source of income. To get started in this work, connection can be made with a photographer, who can suggest leads and who is often willing to cooperate by actually

189

GOOD SOURCE OF INCOME. Air-painting of portraits offers one of many good sources of income. Portraits of children and babies are the most saleable form of this work. They are easy to air-brush in natural colors, and when well executed, they can command good prices.

taking orders for the artist. Portraits of children and babies are the most saleable form of this work. They are easy to air-brush in natural colors, and when well executed, they can command good prices.

Photo-engravers, too, have need for services of the air-brush artist for various kinds of work. Regular accounts can be established with the smaller engraving companies who do not have their own staff artists.

The air-painted mural is being introduced in many public and private buildings, in churches, lodge headquarters, stores, and homes. The artist can make his services known to contractors, architects and interior decorators in his city, so that when they have opportunities to supply work of this nature, they can notify him. The decorating of night clubs, hotels, country clubs, athletic clubs, and similar quarters can include murals and wall decorations made with the air brush.

Neighborhood theatres that employ no staff display artists are possible outlets for air-brushed poster portraits to advertise coming and current attractions. Their usually low advertising budgets might not make possible elaborate hand-painted posters, but the air-brush artist might be able to do the work at a more attractive price, considering the speed and ease with which he can work. Regular accounts can be created in this way. In every community of any size there is a little theatre organization that gives plays for local benefits. These organizations can make good use of air-brushed portraits and posters to portray outstanding players and to advertise coming presentations.

The versatile air-brush artist can sometimes obtain commissions at conventions to make large caricatures or air-brushed portraits of leading individuals. They can be made in large scale for display in the assembly hall or other central location.

THE SALARIED ARTIST. This is the day of specialists. The air-brush artist is a specialist in his particular form of art execution. The saying is that there is always a demand for a specialist—if he is a good specialist, and this is as true in air-brush art as in any other vocation. Even the work of an air-brush specialist is in turn divided into classifications that require special training.

The salary of the air-brush artist depends upon his ability, the size of the organization for whom he works, and the particular position he holds on the art staff. Art directors and head layout artists generally receive the top salaries, and their first assistants usually receive the next highest salaries.

The air-brush artist, however, is a specialist in his own right, and he can accordingly command a salary commensurate with his training, his ability, and the form of work in which he is especially proficient.